Hindu Dharma and Sanskriti

Hindu Dharma and Sanskriti

Dr. Sadanand Damodar Sapre

PRABHAT PAPERBACKS

Published by
PRABHAT PAPERBACKS
An imprint of Prabhat Prakashan Pvt. Ltd.
4/19 Asaf Ali Road,
New Delhi-110002 (INDIA)
e-mail: prabhatbooks@gmail.com

ISBN 978-93-90900-26-8
HINDU DHARMA AND SANSKRITI
by Dr. Sadanand Damodar Sapre

Edition
First, 2022

Price
₹ 200.00 (Rupees Two Hundred only)

Printed at
R-Tech Offset Printers, Delhi

PROLOGUE

There are several confusions regarding Hindu Dharma and Hindu Sanskriti. An effort has been made in this book to address them, apart from their brief description/explanation. The compiler of the book (who is not the author) is not an *authority* in this field, he is rather a *layman*; but this has helped him in identifying the difficulties faced by a common human being in understanding these complex but very important and essential concepts.

Various books available on the subject and the speeches and writings of some of the eminent personalities who are great authorities in this field are major sources for this compilation. The compiler expresses his deep sense of gratitude to all of them, in particular to **Shri Ranga Hari**, who has been very kind to go through the manuscript despite his advanced age and gave invaluable suggestions.

The compiler is fully aware that everything he knows is solely because of his family, his school/ college education, the learned persons—social workers—spiritual personalities and many others. He is indebted to one and all.

The language of this book has been purposefully chosen as English. The compiler has travelled in many countries and had interaction with youths everywhere. He has observed that most of them want to know more about Hindu Dharma and Hindu Sanskriti, and this trend is on the rise. Unfortunately, they are well versed mostly only in English, not even in their own mother tongue. Same is the scenario in Bharat among the youths who are under the influence of the day by day increasing importance given to education in English medium. The compiler has experienced in his travels all over Bharat that they too are taking keen interest in Hindu Dharma and Sanskriti. Therefore, the need of hour is, more and more books on Hindu Dharma and Sanskriti should be written in English.

There are no Proper synonyms in English for the words like *Dharma, Sanskriti, Moksha, Guru etc.* which are to be used frequently while dealing with the subject of Hindu Dharma and Sanskriti. The synonyms in English for these words do not give their exact meaning because the Western world doesn't have the conception of the sentiments and feelings expressed in them. For this reason, such words have been used as they are, without translation. The meaning of these keywords has been explained at their first appearance (or at an appropriate place) in this book. Hopefully, this will help readers in having clarity.

The present generation believes more in *rational thinking* rather than in having *faith*. Therefore, they want logical and scientific explanation for the things they don't understand. Also, they feel at home with short descriptions/explanations rather than lengthy ones. Keeping this in mind, the books on this topic should be written in a *reader-friendly* way.

In view of above, the size of the book has been kept as small as possible, without going too much into details. The examples to explain various phenomena have been taken mostly from day-to-day life for easy understanding. (*Sometimes they may not represent the* "exact/appropriate meaning" *of the phenomenon, but help in understanding it.*) It is hoped that this will make the book suitable for everyone, particularly the youths. Moreover, as per the present trend, this has made it short, simple and readable; something similar to a *level-0* book. The readers desiring to know more about the subject are requested to refer to some high-level books.

The first chapter deals with the basic principles of Hindu Dharma, the second chapter with the scientific nature of Hindu Dharma and the third with the Hindu Sanskriti. At some places, the compiler has given comparative analysis of *Hindu Dharma—Semitic religions, Hindu philosophy—Western philosophy, Sanskara—brain washing and some pairs of words,* in view of practical understanding of the subject.

It is hoped that this book will be useful to everyone, in particular to those who are concerned about and working for Hindu Dharma and Sanskriti.

The suggestions of the readers are welcome.

—Dr. Sadanand Damodar Sapre

ACKNOWLEDGEMENTS

The compiler is immensely fortunate to have many young friends who contributed to this book by way of discussion, giving suggestions, making queries, providing useful reference books, typing, getting printouts, dealing with the computer-internet related problems etc. They include Sarva Shri Saumitra Gokhale, Ram Vaidya, Anil Vartak, A. P. Ambalavanan, Sundara Raman, Yogeshwar Dixit, Suresh Jain, Neeraj Dixit, Vishnu Kant, Dhirendra Chaturvedi, Vishwas Chouhan, Surendra Thakre, Kamlesh Patel, Pa. Santosh, C. C. Selvan, K. R. Randeep, K. R. Jayakrishnan, Chandrasekharan K. M., Kishan Gupta, Prem Kumar, Manjesh Kumar Hanawal, Satish Rajput, Ss Lalita Gupta, Ss Alpana Pandey and many more.

The family members have also contributed. They include Vivek (son), Purva (daughter in law), Vandana (daughter), Anurag (son in law), Akhilesh (nephew), Ashutosh Sahasrabuddhe (nephew) and Gauri Hardikar (daughter in law).

The compiler experienced pleasant surprises during his rail travels. When he was working on the printouts of the manuscript, many of the co-passengers took keen interest in them (youth outnumbering the elderly ones). Their inquisitiveness helped the compiler in identifying the portions of the book which needed extra attention.

Most of the above mentioned (with or without name) are matured beyond their years—an encouraging sign of very bright future of our society and nation. The compiler expresses his gratitude towards all of them.

—Dr. Sadanand Damodar Sapre

Contents

1

HINDU DHARMA

(BASIC PRINCIPLES)

INTRODUCTION

DHARMA and **RELIGION** are altogether different conceptions. (Even as per the Oxford dictionary, 'DHARMA' means *'eternal law of Universe'* whereas 'RELIGION' means *'a particular way of worship and faith'*.) Most of the problems and confusions existing today are consequences of taking them as *synonyms*.

The word 'DHARMA' is derived from the root of the word (Dhatu) ***'dhR' (Dhri/Dhru)*** in Sanskrit, whose meaning is ***'Dhriyate Lokah Anena'*** (because of which the Universe is held together) or ***'Dharati Lokam Waa'*** (one which holds the Universe).

The word 'RELIGION' is derived from the Latin word 'RELIGARE' which means ***'to bind together'***. The religion binds the followers to a set of beliefs and behaviours.

Thus, the difference between *Dharma* and *Religion*[1] is somewhat similar to that between *holding together* and *binding together*. In *holding*, the individuals are held together with their identities (including their faiths) kept intact, like a '*salad*'. Moreover, in *Dharma*, it is not just holding together the individuals, it is holding the entire Universe. Thus, the '*canvas*' of *Dharma* is much larger than just the human beings; it covers the entire Universe. On the other hand, in *binding*, the individuals are bound to come together even at the loss of their identities (including their faiths), like a thing that happens in a '*melting pot*'. It can be seen that, the '*canvas*' of religion is confined only to the human beings.

In Vedas and other ancient literature, the words ***'Dharma'*** and ***'Rtam' (Ritam/Rutam)*** have been used with the same meaning. Initially, the word 'Ritam' has been used more frequently than the word 'Dharma'; but, from Purana time onwards till the present time, the word 'Dharma' is predominantly in use. The word 'Ritam' has been confined mostly to some Mantras/hymns of *Shruti*[2]. However, the

---

1. The most appropriate Sanskrit word for *religion* is ***Matam***, although there are two more words for it—***Pantha*** and ***Sampradaya***.
2. *The Vedas and Upanishadas fall in the category of 'Shruti'*—'that which has been heard'. *They are considered*

meaning of *'Ritam'* and *'Dharma'* is the same. They are not like the words *'Dharma'* and *'religion'*, whose meanings are different.

The word DHARMA has several other meanings[3] as well and therefore, its meaning depends on the context. However, when human beings lead their lives in accordance with these meanings; the result

---

as impersonal/authorless (Apaurusheya), because the Rishis (sages) and Rishikas (female Rishis) have heard them in the state of trance (Samadhi) directly from the Supreme Being (God). They are known as 'seers' (Drashta), who compiled them. (It should be noted that apart from several Rishis, many Rishikas like Gargi, Maitreyi, Ghosha, Lopamudra etc. have also contributed in their compilation.) *They consist of revelation and eternal truth. Other ancient literature like Manusmriti (also known as 'Manav Dharma Shastra'), Naradasmriti, Parasarasmriti, Devalasmriti, Dharmasutra, Ramayana, Mahabharata, Shad Darshan (6 philosophies), Ashtadash (18) Puranas etc. fall in the category of 'Smriti'*—'that which has been remembered'. *These have been written by sages like Narada, Parasara, Valmiki, Vyasa, Gautam, Kanada, Kapil etc. 'Shruti' and 'Smriti' are considered as primary text and secondary text respectively. The former is considered as superior among the two. However, the Bhagavad Gita has been given the status of a 'Shruti', although it is a part of Mahabharata (a 'Smriti').*

3. Two of the MEANINGS OF DHARMA are: ***'Dhaaran Karana'*** (to hold, to sustain and maintain) and ***'Jod Ke Rakhana'*** (to keep together).

is always coordination *(Samanvaya)* everywhere, all the time. There is no conflict (*Sangharsha*) anywhere, any time.

In order to achieve this, the human beings must possess certain qualities, they must follow certain rules and dos-don'ts. Hence, all of these qualities are also considered as the meanings of Dharma. Though they themselves are not Dharma, they are the ones who express, promote and strengthen Dharma. *For example*:

- The meaning of Pitri-Dharma/Putra-Dharma is not the religion of father/son, it is their duty (Kartavya). Hence, one meaning of Dharma is ***'Duty'*—Kartavya Dharma**[4].

---

4. The categories of *Kartavya Dharma* are:
   (A) *Relationship based*—Duty of father, son, brother, family members etc. {Respectively Pitri (father) Dharma, Putra (son) Dharma, Bhratri (brother) Dharma, Kul (family) Dharma etc.}
   (B) *Geographical*—Duty towards neighbour, native village, nation etc. {Respectively Pados (neighbour) Dharma, Gram (village) Dharma, Rashtra (nation) Dharma etc.}
   (C) *Work/occupation (Karma) based*—Duty of ruler, ruled, soldier, professional etc. {Respectively Raj (ruler) Dharma, Praja (ruled) Dharma, Sainik (soldier) Dharma, Vyavasaaya (profession) Dharma etc.}

- The Government makes certain laws (Vidhi) to control anarchy, theft, dacoity, corruption, discrimination, violence etc. and to ensure discipline, harmony, safety, peace, progress, feeling of oneness, national integration etc. The society can't move on smoothly without these laws. Hence, one meaning of Dharma is **'*Law*'—Vidhi Dharma**.

  [One should understand the difference between *'Governed by law'* and *'Governed by Dharma'*. In the first case, the laws are followed mostly because of *fear* of the state machinery which can give some punishment; but in absence of such fear, they are likely to be broken. On the other hand, it is *voluntary* in the second case—comes from within—and hence laws are not broken even when there is no such *fear*. Thus, for a *Dharmik* person (one who follows Dharma), Dharma is beyond the law.]
- Unity, harmony, cooperation, friendship, honesty, good character, forgiveness, speaking truth, non-violence, keeping

---

(D) *Other*—Yatayat (traffic) Dharma, Gathabandhan (coalition) Dharma, Paryavaran (environment) Dharma etc.

promises etc. are very essential for every human being. All of these virtues can be broadly categorised as morality (Naitikata). Hence, one meaning of Dharma is ***'Morality'* —Naitik Dharma**.

- When a beggar begs 'Dharam {he means 'Dharma'} Do Maa' (Oh mother, kindly give me Dharma), he is not asking for religion; he is asking for charity (Daana). Hence, one meaning of Dharma is ***'Charity'*—Daana Dharma**.
- Dharmarth Dawakhana (hospital) does not mean a hospital for religion or religious purpose; it is a hospital where the treatment of the patients is free of cost, a type of service (Sewa) for the deprived people. Hence, one meaning of Dharma is ***'Service'*—Sewa Dharma**.

ANOTHER MEANING OF 'DHARMA' IS:

'*Basic* (or *Natural*) Characteristic—Prakriti Dharma'. The entire animate world (*except the human beings*) and inanimate world follow the Prakriti Dharma. Thus, 'Hasti (elephant) Dharma' does not mean the religion of an elephant, it is the basic characteristics of an elephant. Similarly, the meaning of 'Jala (water) Dharma' is not the religion of water, it is the basic characteristic of water, which is *'To flow'*.

[*Looking at the several meanings of '**Dharma**' explained above, it appears that the nearest word for it in English is '**Righteousness**'.*]

Quotations/Logos that include the word *Dharma* can be seen at several important places in Bharat like Lok Sabha (lower house of parliament)—*Dharmachakra Pravartanaya,* Rajya Sabha (upper house of parliament)—*Satyam Vada Dharmam Chara,* Supreme Court—*Yato Dharmastato Jayah,* EME Corps of Military—*Karmah Hi Dharmah,* ...... and nowhere the meaning of *Dharma* is *Religion.*

The word ***Secular*** was included in the preamble of the Constitution of Bharat in the mid-seventies. It should be noted that the Hindi version of the Constitution has used the word ***Pantha****nirapeksha* for the word ***Secular*** (rather than using the word ***Dharma****nirapeksha*).

FUNCTIONS and FEATURES OF DHARMA

The *Functions* of Dharma are given as:

(1) ***'Dhaaranaat Dharma Ityahuh***
Dharmo Dhaarayati Prajaah
Yasyaat Dhaaranasanyuktah
Sa Dharma Iti Nishchayah'

(The one which sustains people is Dharma and everything with the capability of sustaining people is also Dharma). Thus, one of the functions of Dharma is *sustaining people*.

(2) ***'Yatah AbhyudayaNihshreyasaSiddhih Sa Dharmah'***

(The one which yields material and spiritual prosperity is Dharma). Thus, another function of Dharma is *material and spiritual prosperity of people*. [For this reason, ***'spirituality'*** (realisation of 'oneness' with every soul and with everything that exists in the Universe) is also a major aspect of *Dharma* along with ***'materialism'***.]

The eternal law of the Universe is coordination/harmony, not conflict; which can be seen everywhere in the Universe. It is applicable to the entire animate and inanimate creation {who follow their own Prakriti Dharma (Hasti-Dharma, Jala-Dharma etc.)}, a fact that can be seen everywhere on earth. The only exception is the human being, who, because of his/her mind and intellect, can behave with or without discretion, resulting in a Dharmik (as per Dharma) behaviour or an Adharmik (against Dharma) behaviour. Hence, harmony on earth can be maintained only if the human beings lead their entire life by following certain rules, laws, dos-don'ts etc. This, in essence, is their Dharma.

All of these rules, laws etc. have been observed, understood and realised by the people known as Hindu and hence, ***Dharma*** is known as ***Hindu Dharma***. However, these rules-laws etc. are applicable to every human being ***(Manav)*** all over the world ***(Vishwa)***, not confined only to Hindus. (Einstein was the first person to observe and understand the law of relativity and hence, it is known as '*Einstein's law of relativity*'; but it is applicable to everyone, not confined only to his country persons or the people belonging to his religion.) Hence, ***Hindu Dharma*** is ***Manav Dharma*** or ***Vishwa Dharma***—the global ethics applicable to the entire humankind.

The word ***Sanatana*** is a combination of two words: ***Sana*** (old) and ***Tana*** (new). Hence, its meaning is ***'although old, ever new'*** or ***'ever present, ever evolving'***. It is said that sunrise is Sanatana because although it is *ever present*, it is also ever new/evolving. Like sunrise, Dharma is also Sanatana because the *eternal law of the Universe*—Dharma—is *ever present* as well as *ever new/evolving*. Hence, another name for Dharma is ***Sanatana Dharma***.

Thus, ***DHARMA*** is ***HINDU DHARMA*** or ***MANAV DHARMA*** or ***VISHWA DHARMA*** or ***SANATANA DHARMA***.

[The meaning of the word ***Sanatani*** (which is derived from the word Sanatana) is not *conservative* or *one who always looks in the past*, as is usually taken; it is ***"one who looks in the past*** (to take inspiration and learn) ***but is aware of the present as well*** (to tackle the contemporary issues)".]

In Hindu Dharma, ten virtues have been expressed as the *features* (Lakshan) of Dharma in the following *Shloka*:

"Dhrutih Kshama Damosteyam
ShauchamIndriyanigrahah
DheerVidya SatyamAkrodhah
Dashakam Dharmalakshanam"

[Dhruti *(Dhairya/patience)*, Kshama *(forgiveness)*, Dama *(Sanyam/restraint)*, Asteya *(not stealing anything)*, Shaucha (*inner and outer cleanliness/ sanctity*), Indriyanigraha *(control over the organs of sense)*, Dhee *(intelligence/wisdom)*, Vidya *(knowledge)*, Satya *(truthfulness)* and Akrodha *(absence of anger)*—these are the ten *features* of Dharma.]

It may be noted that all of these ten virtues are essential for every human being to maintain harmony, irrespective of their religious creed.

It may also be noted that even an Astik (*a believer in the existence of God - the Supreme Being and one who believes in the authority of Vedas as revelations; can be called as a 'theist')* is considered as *Adharmik,* if he/she does not possess these virtues (e.g. Rawana of Ramayana, who was an ardent devotee of Shiva—one of the Hindu deities); whereas a *Nastik (a non-believer in the existance of God and one who does not believe in the authority of Vedas as revelations; can be called as an 'atheist')* is considered as *Dharmik,* if he/she possesses these virtues (e.g. Rishi Kanada, a great saint of ancient times who was a non-believer in God, but was a great scientist as well, who invented the *Atomic Theory* given in his invaluable treatise *Vaisheshik Darshan,* which is extremely useful for the human race).

BRAHMAN

One of the basic principles of Hindu Dharma is the conception of one ***BRAHMAN***, which is *root and cause* of the existence of the entire universe. **[***BRAHMAN should not be confused with the word BRAAHMAN (BRAAHMIN), one of the four Varnas (classification of society) of Hindu Dharma.***]** Brahman is the universal soul suffusing all creation. It has no beginning, no end. It is all pervading, omnipresent, omnipotent and omniscient. It is transcendental, eternal and infinite. It is free of any attribute (Nirguna) and with no form or shape (Nirakara).

[The meaning of the word *BRAHMAN* is *infinitely expanding*. It is the *consciousness existing infinitely around*. Brahman is referred to in neuter gender **'It'.]**

Brahman is addressed by people as Bhagawan, Ishwar, Deva, Devi, Wahe Guru, Almighty, God, Lord, Allah or by other names; but the meaning is the same - **the Ultimate Being, the Absolute, the root and cause of everything.**

It is believed that initially there was existence of only Brahman and a desire germinated into its mind—"**Ekoham Bahusyam**" (I am one, want to become many). That's how the entire creation came into being but in each and every creation, there is Brahman. (It's something like **magnetism**. When a magnet is broken in several pieces, each piece has magnetism in it.) At the end, everything will merge in Brahman. Thus, ***ALL comes forth from Brahman and ALL returns to Brahman***.

Usually, it is said—"***Unity in Diversity***". However, the problem with this phrase is that '*Diversity*' is assumed to be the basic fact and '*Unity*' is searched in it. The Hindu philosophy says that "***Oneness manifests in Diversity***". Thus, there is '*one*' single element (Brahman) in the entire creation and '*many*' are its manifestations.

The conception of one Brahman in entire creation has resulted in a typical mindset of Hindus

to accept, appreciate and enjoy all diversities present in the universe and this is one of the main features of Hindu Dharma and Sanskriti.

The significance of the Hindu tradition of greeting each other by "*Namaste*" (which is becoming popular all over the world—as one of the '*new normal*'—after the Covid-19 pandemic) is "*I bow to the divinity within you*".

The Hindu belief that there is *one element* (*Brahman*) in each and every thing, is being reflected in the popular saying "***Kan Kan Mein Bhagawan***"—*Brahman/God* is present in each and every particle, i.e. God is present everywhere. Hence one should see God in everything. (Now the West has also accepted the same principle in the form of '*God particle*' and the Nobel Prize has been conferred on the physicist Leon Lederman in the year 1988.)

[It's an irony that the Hindus who believe in *Kan Kan Mein Bhagwan,* began to consider their own people belonging to the so-called lower castes as untouchables, which resulted in several social atrocities on them. It is laudable that now the Hindu society is doing atonement (*in the form of reservation and some special provisions to uplift them*) for this *heinous sin,* because as the American President Abraham Lincoln has said about *slavery*—"*If* ***slavery*** *in not wrong, then nothing in the world is wrong*"—the same can be said about ***untouchability*****.]**

Brahman can be imagined as something *akin* to pure energy, which has no form or shape, but can manifest itself in numerous forms and shapes that can be perceived with some of our senses (*although, energy can't be*). Brahman is somewhat similar to this phenomenon. However, it should be clearly understood that energy is a part of Brahman, whereas Brahman is much more than pure energy. It is the *Supreme Consciousness which pervades the entire universe.*

It is extremely difficult to visualise the Brahman which is free of any attribute and without any shape. A common human being needs its symbolic representation. Therefore, the Hindus have visualised several ***Deities*** {they are referred to as *Brahman with attributes* (Saguna Brahman) or *personal God/ Goddess*}, who can be seen and worshipped. However, all of them represent the one Brahman. ***Deity-worship* is 'worshiping the Brahman through the deity'; not just 'worshiping the deity'**. Thus, the existence of several deities does not make the Hindus *polytheists* who believe in several Gods. The deities are many ways to think about God, the Brahman. Their names and forms are different, but the reality is the same—the one Brahman.

It is to be noted that most of the people who do not need anything to visualise Brahman are also deity worshippers, because it helps in attaining self-realisation, having concentration, stabilising and purifying one's mind and for contemplation and meditation. It also helps in getting rid of one's weaknesses and bad tendencies.

In Hindu Dharma, one can find the conception of ***feminine deities.*** They are referred to as ***'Sarvamangala Mangalyam'***. (Perhaps because of the divine femininity, the heart of a Hindu is usually full of compassion, kindness and love.)

During the Vedic times, the divinities have been Indra (king of Gods), Mitra (sun), Varuna (God of ocean), Agni (fire), Aditi (Goddess who is personification of infinity) etc. Later on, many great personalities were added to it (Rama, Krishna, Laxmi, Parvati, Saraswati etc.) and the process of adding new ones is still continuing. (Hanumana, Ganesha, Dattatreya, Murugana/Subramanya/Kartikeya, Vitthala, Ayyappa, Santoshi Mata etc.)

RELIGION

The human race has passed through various stages during evolution of life on earth, starting from the primitive stage and arrived at the modern stage with fully grown mind and intellect. Since then, several questions regarding their individual existence, the existence of the Universe, the creator and the path to reach Him/It, and the ultimate truth of human life are wandering in their minds. The important ones among them have been :

1. Who am I?
2. Wherefrom I came?
3. What is the purpose of my life?
4. Where will I go?
5. What is the Universe?
6. Wherefrom it came?
7. What is its purpose?
8. Where will it go?
9. Who is the creator?
10. How can one realise and reach the creator?

***Science* is unable to give full and proper answers to such questions; because it can give answers only to the question "*how*?", not to the question "*why*?". However, *spirituality* can give full and proper answers to them.**

There have been several great spiritual personalities all over the world who have given full and proper answers to such questions, particularly about the *root and cause* (known as Brahman, God etc.) of the existence of each and everything. Moreover, they have shown a path to realise and reach the root and cause. They had a tremendous impact on the people around, who began to follow them and the number of followers began to grow. Such groups of people have their own identity which is known as ***Religion*** with a specific name. (Jain, Bauddha, Shaiva, Vaishnava, Sikh, Christian, Muslim etc.)

Religion can be classified as:

1. Founder based. (Jain, Bauddha, Christian, Muslim, Sikh etc.)
2. Deity based. (Shaiva, Vaishnava, Ganapatya, Shakta etc.)

[*It should be noted that most of the present day Hindus who fall in the "Deity based" category, are "believers in all or several deities, not just one".*]

Another classification of religion may be:

1. Religions originated in Bharat (Shaiva, Vaishnava, Ganapatya, Shakta, Jain, Bauddha, Sikh etc.) and
2. Religions originated outside Bharat. The prominent among the second category are the ***Semitic Religions***[5]. They need to be studied in details.

---

5. The name of the eldest son of the mythological character *Noah* is *Sem* and his descendant race is known as *Semitic race*. Their religions (*Judaism, Christianity-Christian, Islam-Muslim*) are known as '*Semitic religions*' (also known as '*Abrahamic religions*'—named after the Prophet Abraham).

[There are other religions like Shinto, Tao, Confucianism, Zoroastrianism etc. and traditional indigenous religions like Druid, Maori, Aboriginal, Zulu, Dinka, Native American etc. which can be seen in different parts of the world. They are having many similarities with Hindu Dharma. Therefore, they need not be studied in details like the Semitic religions.]

While understanding the ***Hindu Dharma***[6], it is extremely important to understand the Semitic religions, in particular *Christianity* and *Islam*, because they are the widely followed Semitic religions, which are by nature *expansionist* (rigorously involved in religious conversion, because, in their opinion, theirs is the *only true religion* and *true God*, and hence it is their *God-given sacred duty* to convert the people of other religions to their religion). **[***More on this at later stages in this book.***]** The third Semitic religion—

---

6. In a way, '*Hindu Dharma*' may also be referred to as *"Hindu religion***s***"* or *"Dharmik religion***s***"* or *"a league of religion***s***"* as it encompasses all religions originated in Bharat, such as Shaiva, Vaishnava, Ganapatya, Shakta, Jain, Bauddha, Sikh etc. which are Dharma based. **[**It should be remembered that Dr. B. R. Ambedkar, who presented the '*Hindu Code Bill*' in the Parliament of Bharat in early fifties as the then Union Law Minister, included not only the conventional Hindus (Shaiva, Vaishnava, Ganapatya, Shakta etc. who are usually considered as Hindus), but the Sikh, Bauddha and Jain as well under the word '*Hindu*' appearing in the name of the bill.**]**

Judaism—is less aggressive, perhaps because of very small number of its followers and their very strict and difficult process to convert to Judaism.

Usually, a Hindu comes across a Christian or a Muslim every now and then (because of their very large number in the world) and he/she is likely to get confused regarding several things. He/she may even fall prey to religious conversion.

A comparative study of ***Hindu Dharma*** (HD) and ***Semitic Religions*** (SR) may help in clearing some doubts and having more clarity.

- In HD, God is omnipresent and one can talk, realise and reach God. One can even become a God (*Nara Se Narayana*); whereas, in SR, God is considered as living in heaven and no one can talk, realise and reach *Him*. For that, one needs a messenger/mediator like Moses or Jesus or Prophet.
- In HD, there are many deities (including feminine deities), but the entire human race is undivisible; whereas in SR, there is only one God (who is masculine), but the entire human race is divided into two categories—believers and non-believers.
- The HD is free from any *dogma*, whereas dogma lies at the core of SR. For this reason,

it is not proper to address Hindu Dharma as *Hinduism*, because *ism* stands for a closed book of thoughts or a set of dogmas, and Hindu Dharma is free from any dogma.

[The word *Hinduism* has been used for *Hindu Dharma* by many great scholars and spiritual personalities to explain it to the people who do not understand the meaning of the word *Dharma*. However, during further elaboration, they have made it very clear that it is free from any dogma.

The word *Hinduism* is also used for *Hindutva*, which is not proper for the same reason—*ism* stands for a set of dogmas. *Hinduness* is a more appropriate word for *Hindutva*.]

- Hindu Religions are *religions of realisation*, whereas the Semitic Religions are *religions of belief*.
- In HD, the focus is on *conduct*; whereas in SR, it is on *faith*.
- In HD, the key word is *ALSO;* whereas in SR, it is *ONLY*. [This has been discussed in the next section of this chapter.]
- In HD, the human being is considered as a virtuous human being (*Punyatma*); whereas in SR, the human being is considered as a *consequence of sin*.

- In HD, the *Moksha* (ultimate liberation) is *achieved by an individual*; whereas in SR, it is *given by God*.
- In HD, there are many treatises and they explain various phenomena rationally and logically, and awaken the consciousness and discretion of the human beings. A person need not have faith in all of them and in everything mentioned in them. They are not taken as unquestionable. One can even go beyond them to attain self-realisation. On the other hand, the treatises of SR (only one in each of them) are full of dogmas and in a way, they compel one to accept everything mentioned in them either because of the fear of hell or allures of heaven. They are taken as unquestionable. One who questions them is not tolerated and is considered as a *heretic*[7] who is to be punished.
- In HD, the sainthood is conferred on noble persons by the *society* during their life for their selfless spiritual/social services; whereas in SR, it is given to a person by a *committee* only after his/her death, who has

7. It is to be noted that there are no synonyms in Sanskrit for the words like *heretic, heresy, heathen and blasphemy*.

served the religion and one of the essential conditions for this *canonisation* is that at least one miracle should be attributed to him/her.

Religion has played a key role in making the **Dharma** as important as it is. It inculcates various virtues, instils good values among the followers and helps them stay away from evil qualities. Religion has tremendous impact over a human mind, which can be seen not only in the entire life of its followers, but also in their intense wish for the last rites to be performed as per their religion after their death, even if they die in some other country.

Dharma is universal, but religion is a sort of personal matter. An individual should be allowed to choose and follow a religion of his/her choice and perform its rites. At the same time, a person belonging to a religion should not be expected/compelled to follow any other religion and perform its rites. *(e.g. a Jain should not be expected/compelled to follow the Bauddha religion and perform its rites, a Shaiva should not be expected/compelled to follow the Vaishnava religion and perform its rites, a Muslim should not be expected/compelled to follow the Christian religion and perform its rites and so on).* However, **everyone should respect other religions and their rites.**

ENTITIES OF THE UNIVERSE

There are ***four entities*** in the Universe:

1. ***Vyashti*** (individual)
2. ***Samashti*** (society—which is a collective existence of human beings)
3. ***Srishti*** (creation) and
4. ***Parmeshti*** (Almighty—the primordial cosmic energy of creation).

A person has to lead his/her entire life in such a way that coordination/harmony among all of these four entities is maintained everywhere, all the time; resulting in happiness. For this, he/she has to perform his/her duties and follow certain rules, laws, dos-don'ts etc. This is *Dharma (Hindu Dharma/ Manav Dharma/Vishwa Dharma/Sanatana Dharma).*

The *Dharma* regarding the first three entities (Vyashti, Samashti and Srishti) is in toto applicable to the entire human race. [e.g. taking care of one's body {Shareer (body) Dharma under Vyashti Dharma}, follow the traffic rules {Yatayat (traffic) Dharma under Samashti Dharma}, harvesting of natural resources (Dohan) rather than exploitation (Shoshan) of nature under Srishti Dharma.]

The *Dharma* regarding the fourth entity (Parameshti) is *religion* (this can be referred to as

Moksha Dharma), which helps a human being to reach Brahman and one enters the realm of spirituality. This need not be the same for all, but a mindset is essential whereby one accepts the *existence of Brahman in several forms* and hence one believes in ***'Ekam Sat Vipraah Bahudha Vadanti'***[8]**.** (*That which exists is* **One**, *wise persons call* **It** *by various names.* It is to be noted that the meaning of 'Sat' in this Mantra is 'that which exists', which is usually taken as 'truth'.) This mindset is helpful in accepting the existence of other paths (religions) to reach ***Brahman*** and hence, there is no conflict among various religions. This ensures harmony. **[***It can be seen that a Hindu usually bows down his/her head in respect, whenever he/she sees a place of worship of other religions (like a Mosque or a Church) or their sacred place/symbol (like a Majaar or*

---

8. The full Mantra of Rigved (1/164/46) is—
   "Indram Mitram Varunam Agnim Ahuh
   Atho Divyah Saa Suparno Garutman
   Ekam Sat Vipraah Bahudha Vadanti
   Agnim Yamam Matarishwanam Ahuh"
   [One invokes and worships **It** in the form of Indra, Mitra, Varuna and Agni. **It** also exists in the form of Garutman (eagle)—the divine golden-feathered big bird. ***That which exists is* One, *wise persons call* It *by various names***; whether this invocation is for Agni, Yama (deity of justice) or Matarishwan (Vayu—*gas*).**]**

a crucified Jesus Christ).]

To have this kind of mindset, one has to believe in what can be referred to, only for understanding purpose, as ***'ALSOism'*** (the mindset that says 'I am right, you are *ALSO* right', 'I am good, you are *ALSO* good', 'I will get ultimate liberation (Moksha), you will *ALSO* get it'), which is by nature *INCLUSIVE*; in place of ***'ONLYism'*** (the mindset that says '*ONLY* I am right, you are wrong', '*ONLY* I am good, you are bad', '*ONLY* I will get ultimate liberation, you will not'), which is by nature *EXCLUSIVE.* [Swami Vivekananda has categorically mentioned in his historic *1893 Chicago Speech* that there is no synonym in Sanskrit for the word '*exclusion*'.]

The ALSOism leads not only to ***tolerance*** but also to ***universal acceptance***, which in turn, leads to ***Samaadara*** (equal respect to all) resulting in harmony ('*live and let live*' type of thinking); whereas the ONLYism leads to ***intolerance***, often resulting in ***fanaticism***, which in turn, results in conflict, bloodshed, massacre and even genocide; as can be seen in the entire human history.

[It may be noted that the '*basic thinking*' in tolerance and intolerance is the same. {'*ONLY* I am right, you are wrong', '*ONLY* I am good, you are bad',

'*ONLY* I will get ultimate liberation, you will not'.} The difference is only in its *manifestation*. In tolerance, it is '...... but I will tolerate you' whereas in intolerance, it is '...... hence, I will not tolerate you'. Thus, although tolerance is better than intolerance, it is not good enough. Samaadara is the kind of mindset that is needed.]

Each religion should teach *ALSOism* to its followers, which will result in the mindset of *Samaadara;* rather than teaching *ONLYism,* resulting in the mindset of *intolerance*. (The religious leaders can play a vital role in this.) It would help in establishing world peace.

DHARMAYUDDHA and DHARMARAJYA

Sometimes, a ***'Dharmayuddha'*** is considered the same as a ***'Crusade'*** or a ***'Jihad'***, but this is not proper. The Crusade or Jihad is fought to save or expand a particular religion and thus, it is a war between two religions. On the other hand, the Dharmayuddha is a Yuddha (war) between Dharma and A-Dharma. (*It should be remembered that 'Dharma' is not 'religion' and the 'Dharmayuddha' is not 'a war between two religions'.*) The war of Mahabharata is known as a Dharmayuddha because it was a war between Dharma and A-Dharma, represented by Pandavas and Kauravas respectively, who belonged to the same family.

Sometimes, a ***'Dharmarajya'*** is considered the same as a ***'theocratic state'***, but this as well is not proper. In a *theocratic state,* the people belonging to a particular religion do possess a *special status* as compared to the people belonging to other religions; something which is against the *concept* of a ***'secular state'***. (The dictionary meaning of the word '*secular*' is '*of this world*', but the popular meaning of the phrase '*secular state*' is '*a state, where everyone is considered as equal, irrespective of his/ her religion*'.) On the other hand, in a *Dharmarajya,* there is no discrimination among the people based on their religion. So, it is always a secular state. **[***In today's context, a Dharmarajya can be considered as something like a* ***Rule of Law*** *or more precisely a* ***Rule of Moral Law****, where Primary Laws are given in the Constitution and the Secondary Laws are made by the Parliament and/or the State Assemblies in the light of the Primary Laws.***]**

Sometimes, a '***Dharmarajya***' is considered '***anti-democratic***'. Let us analyse this. There has been the rule of kings in the history of Bharat for thousands of years and most of these kingdoms are considered as Dharmarajya.

However, it has never been a ***Dictatorship*** (like that of Hitler/Mussolini/Stalin/Mao/Saddam/Idi Amin), where only one person (the Dictator) takes all decisions and people are forced to accept and follow them, irrespective of their likes and dislikes. On the other hand, during the kingdom period of Bharat, there had always been a council of Ministers and representatives of all sections of people in the form of *Paur, Jaanapad* etc. and the king used to take all decisions after discussing with them. [When king Dasharatha wanted the coronation (Rajyabhisheka) of Rama—making him king during his life itself, he announced his name only after discussing with his ministers and representatives of people.] Thus, **the basic principles of democracy—*'Role of people in decision making'* and *'Acceptance of the Ruled for the Ruler'*—have always been followed in Bharat, including the kingdom period.**

[Sometimes, it is claimed that democracy is the contribution of the West to Bharat. Is it true? Let us see the post 1947 scenario in Bharat and Pakistan (*the Britishers have ruled this entire region up to 1947*) regarding the status of democracy and one gets the answer. The conception of democracy is not alien to Bharat and therefore a healthy democracy exists in it. Pakistan is a creation of anti-Hindu and anti-Bharat sentiments, and everyone can see the status of democracy in that country.]

CHATURVIDHA PURUSHARTHA

In Hindu Dharma, there is a concept of *'four goals of human life'* known as ***'Chaturvidha Purushartha*** (goal of human pursuit)'—**Dharma**, **Artha** (finance/wealth), **Kaama** (desire) and **Moksha**. (There is no appropriate word for *Moksha* in English. The nearest ones are *salvation* or *emancipation*. However, the meaning of *Moksha/Mukti/Nirvaana* is *ultimate/final/spiritual liberation*, when one gets a direct experience of the *Absolute Truth/Reality* and then the *unison/merger with Brahman*.)

Dharma is the primary and most important Purushartha, Artha and Kaama are the innate Purushartha and Moksha is the ultimate goal of human life.

Each human being is composed of two components: (1) *Purusha* (Atman or soul), which is immortal; and (2) *Prakriti* (body), which is perishable. A soul can't express itself without a body and a body is lifeless without a soul. **The goals for the Prakriti part of the human being are Dharma, Artha and Kaama, whereas the goal for the Purusha part is Moksha.**

A person has to lead his/her entire life by following these Purusharthas in such a way that Artha and Kaama are within the ambit of Dharma. This ensures the well-being of ALL. Thereafter one is eligible to achieve Moksha, considered as *the purpose of each individual life*.

Moksha is a state of realisation that an individual is not different from Brahman. {'*Aham Brahmaasmi*'—I am (part of) Brahman.} It should be clearly understood that this is not *conceit*, it is *realisation*; after which there are no desires, no identities, no bondages, no love, no hate, no pride and no feeling of doer-ship. Just the real knowledge of *Self* and *Brahman*, and the existing *non-duality* (Adwaita).

One can easily understand that achieving Moksha is extremely difficult for a human being.

PATHS TO ACHIEVE MOKSHA

In Hindu Dharma, there are mainly three paths to achieve ***Moksha***:

Bhakti Yoga (Path of Devotion)—unconditional and total surrender towards the deity.

Jnana Yoga (Path of Intellect)—to understand and realise the oneness with Brahman.

Karma Yoga (Path of Action)—to fulfil all duties without expecting anything in return.

[Sometimes, ***Raja Yoga***, which is a type of *Yoga* (also known as *Ashtanga Yoga*), is considered as the fourth path to achieve *Moksha*.]

A person can choose any one of the above three paths *OR* a combination of any two paths *OR* a combination of all the three paths, as per his/her liking, mindset and circumstances.

It can be seen that in Bhakti Yoga, one should have full faith and belief in the path (of deity worship), for which there may or may not be a scientific or logical explanation. [*Strictly speaking, Bhakti is also scientific, because it is related to Shraddha* (*Shrat*—with efforts, *Dha*—held) *which is a result of complete analysis and then faith.*] In Semitic religions, this is the only path (*the name may be different*), with deity worship being replaced by prayer (for Jews and Christians) and Ibaadat/Sajdah (for Muslims), to achieve *ultimate liberation*[9]. On the other hand, in Hindu Dharma,

9. There is a provision of Karma Yoga (*the name may be different*) in Semitic religions, but it is not considered as a path to achieve ultimate liberation and Jnana Yoga is almost non-existent in them because of several dogmas.

The paths to achieve ultimate liberation (or something similar) are also given in many religions other than the Semitic religions, but as has been mentioned earlier, they have many similarities with Hindu Dharma and this happens to be one of them.

apart from Bhakti Yoga, there is a provision of Jnana Yoga and Karma Yoga to achieve Moksha, which are very scientific and logical. Thus, in Semitic religions, the ultimate liberation depends only on faith and belief, whereas, in Hindu Dharma, it does not depend solely on faith and belief, there are other ways as well. A truly scientific and practical approach!

SHAASHWAT DHARMA, YUGA DHARMA and AAPAD DHARMA

One of the reasons as to why Hindu Dharma has retained its originality for thousands of years is the concept of Shaashwat (Eternal) Dharma, Yuga (Era *OR* Time-dependent) Dharma and Aapad (Emergency) Dharma.

- ***Shaashwat Dharma***—The basic principles of Dharma, which are eternal in nature.
- ***Yuga Dharma***—The manifestation of Shaashwat Dharma in the context of changing times. (It is also known as *Aachaar Dharma*.)

[To have *true love* among the husband-wife is Shaashwat Dharma. Its manifestation is Yuga Dharma, which may change with time. For example—earlier, it might have been the wife walking two steps behind husband, whereas today, both of them walk together, perhaps holding each other's hand. However, in both the situations, the Shaashwat Dharma of *true love* is a must.]

- ***Aapad Dharma***—Sometimes, it is not possible to follow the Yuga Dharma (based on the Shaashwat Dharma), due to certain emergency-type exceptional situations and therefore, something which is anti-Dharma is to be followed. This is Aapad Dharma. It is to be followed only during emergencies. However, in normal situations, the Yuga Dharma based on the Shaashwat Dharma is to be followed.

[To take bath in order to keep the body clean is Shaashwat Dharma. The actual bathing method, which changes with time {like using Besan (Chana Daal floor) and other such things available in home *OR* using bathing soap *OR* using shampoo, conditioner and other modern things} is Yuga Dharma. During an emergency situation {like hospitalisation *OR* a 2-day rail travel in an unreserved overcrowded bogey}, it is not at all possible to take a bath. This is Aapad Dharma. It is to be noted that not taking bath is allowed only as an Aapad Dharma. However, in normal situations, bath is to be taken.]

□

2

HINDU DHARMA
(SCIENTIFIC NATURE)

INTRODUCTION

Usually, it is assumed that ***Dharma*** (as an incorrect synonym for ***religion***) is a matter of faith and belief, and hence, it is non-scientific; as there is no rationality or logical explanation for most of the things associated with it. If we look at the basic principles of Hindu Dharma from this angle, we find that each one of them has some reasoning behind it. Thus, it can be said that the Hindu Dharma is very scientific in nature, because one of the ways to define science is *"a systematic branch of knowledge, where there is reasoning behind everything and nothing is to be accepted only as a faith or a belief"*.

[It should be noted that although being scientific is *necessary* for Dharma, it is not *sufficient*. Apart from being scientific, Dharma should also be spiritual. Because, as has been seen in the section 'Religion' of the previous chapter, science can give answer to the question 'how', not to the question 'why'. Only spirituality can give answer to this questions. Therefore, Dharma should be scientific as well as spiritual.] •

If we look at the rites, rituals, ceremonies, traditions, practices, faiths, beliefs, festivals etc. associated with 'Hindu Dharma', we find that there is some reasoning behind most of them.

[*Some of the beliefs-rituals followed by Hindus have no or little reasoning behind them. They can be referred to as* ***superstition****. For example—the path crossing by a cat (in particular, a black cat) is considered as a bad omen, the weeping of a dog during night is considered as a bad omen, breaking of crockery is considered as a good omen, putting a small spot of soot (Kaajal) on baby's forehead to save it from* "evil eye", *the rituals like* "bride's brother wrenching the ear of bridegroom" *etc.* ***But, this is human nature and it has nothing to do with Dharma or religion. Moreover, this is not confined only to Hindus. It is a worldwide phenomenon which can be seen in every country and among all religious creeds.*** *Examples of such superstitions* *which are followed in different parts of the world are—13 is considered as an unlucky number* (even in developed countries, the room number sequence in many hotels is 11,12,14,15—the number 13 is not allotted to any room), *considering the number 111 (Nelson) and its multiples as unlucky numbers in cricket, walking under a ladder is considered as a bad omen, looking into a broken mirror is considered as a bad omen, owl hooting is considered as a bad omen, spilling of coffee/tea is considered as a good omen, believing in* "Khamsa" (protection against any form of harm to a person by spreading the right palm in his/her face and by printing the impression of the right palm all over the new possessions like a car or a house), *the rituals like* "new pinch" *and* "same pinch", *and many more such superstitions.*

However, these superstitions should have certain characteristics. (1) They should not be harmful to others. (2) They should be sinless and innocent. (3) They should not be taken as part of a Dharma or a religion. (4) They should be voluntary, not compulsory.

Some of these superstitions help in reducing or removing mental burdens, some of them help in bearing some kind of losses and some of them add much needed 'flavour' to human life.]

DEITY, TRIMURTI and DASHAVATARA

We have already seen in the section BRAHMAN of chapter 1 that it is extremely difficult to visualise the Brahman without any attribute and shape, and therefore, one needs some kind of symbolic representation. For this reason, there is a provision of **deity-worship** in Hindu Dharma. There are several deities, so that a person can worship the deity/deities of his/her own choice or can worship different deities for specific virtues (e.g. Ganesh and Saraswati for intellect, and Hanuman for devotion and might.) However, it should be remembered that *all of them are the manifestations of the BRAHMAN.*

Some of the people do not need any deity for worship, they understand the *Brahman* in their own way (in the form of worshipping nature *or* some symbol like Swastik, Aum etc. *or* some other way). They too fall under Hindu Dharma like the deity worshippers, because of the ***'Spiritual Liberty'*** (everyone having full liberty to choose his/her own way to reach the Brahman) in it. Many tribes, Arya Samaj, Brahmo Samaj and many individuals fall in this category.

The conception of ***Trimurty***—*Brahmaa* (One who creates. It should not be confused with the word *Brahman*—The Almighty), *Vishnu* (One who sustains), *Mahesha/Shiva/Shankara* (One who dissolves)—matches with the cycle of *creation-sustenance-dissolution* of the Universe.

The conception of ***Dashavatara—Ten Avataras*** (Matsya—fish, Kurma—tortoise, Varaha—boar, ...), apart from being the symbolic/mythological/historical stories of ten Avataras (reincarnation) of Vishnu which inculcate good Sanskaras and moral values, their sequence matches with the sequence of evolution of life on earth and the progression of human race.

OUTLOOK TOWARDS NATURE

While others have the conception of ***'Conquering the Nature'***, the Hindu Dharma teaches to take ***'Darshan of the Nature'***. (The meaning of 'Darshan' is not just *'seeing'*, it is *'seeing a deity or a pious thing/ person'*.) Therefore, every Hindu looks towards nature from this angle. For him/her, a river is not just a source of water, it is *mother of people* (Lokamata), a mountain is not just a tourist destination, it is a *land of God* (Devabhumi)—the main reason for having so many temples in mountains—and so on. Therefore, Hindus worship nature, apart from taking its Darshan.

Many of the deities have their own personal vehicle in the form of an animal or a bird (e.g.

Shiva-bull, Vishnu-eagle, Durga-lion, Saraswati-swan, Ganesha-mouse). Many of the deities are associated with an animal or a species (e.g. Krishna-cow, Dattatreya-dog, Shiva-serpent). Many of the deities are associated with a plant or a tree or a flower (e.g. Vishnu-Tulsi, Shiva-Bilwa, Krishna-Parijata, Dattatreya-Audumbara, Murugana-Champa, Ganesha-Durva).

Hindus are aware about the significance of each and every creature, be it a snake or a scorpion or a donkey or even a lizard. They know their role in environment in the form of being a part of the food chain or in the lives of other creatures.

All of these things help Hindus to become echo-sensitive and as a result, they become more echo-friendly. Moreover, they help in making a mindset of having a harmonious relationship with nature—the entire animate world (including plants and trees) and the inanimate world. Hence, there is always *harvesting the natural resources* (Dohan) rather than the *exploitation* (Shoshan) of nature. [*It is an accepted fact that most of the problems related to the environment which the world is facing today are on account of* ***exploitation of nature*** *and the solution lies in* ***harvesting of natural resources***.]

If we look at the things which are considered as very sacred/pious in Hindu Dharma, it can be seen that ***each one of them*** possesses special qualities which are quite unique and useful for humankind. [e.g. **Cow** (its milk and the products like buttermilk, curd, butter, Ghee are very useful and they have some medicinal properties as well; cow-dung is a good pesticide; cow-urine is very useful in making many Ayurvedic medicines), river **Ganga** (because of its self-purifying and non-putrefying properties, it is the only river whose water remains as it is for y ars), plant **Tulsi** (its leaves are very useful during the treatment of illnesses like cough, cold, flu, malaria; many researchers claim that it emits oxygen even during night—a rare phenomenon), ...] This is a result of years (*sometimes generations*) of analytical and scientific study, not just a coincidence or a matter of random selection.

FESTIVALS, PILGRIMAGES and FAIRS

Most of the Hindu festivals/Utsavas {*UTSAVA—UT(remove) SAVA(worldly sorrows), thus the meaning of UTSAVA is "removing the worldly sorrows"*} are related to:

A phenomenon occurring in nature. (Change of season—Makara Sankranti, Makaravilakku, Pongala, Lohri; new year—Varsha Pratipada, Ugadi, Baishagu.)

Related to the environment. (Hariyali Amavas, Karam Puja, Sarhul, Bathukamma.)

Related to river/mountain. (Ganga Dashehara, Pushkaram, Govardhan Puja, Sahyadri Utsav.)

Related to animals/species. (Calf—Vasu Baaras, cattle—Pola, snake cobra—Nag Panchami.)

Related to agriculture. (Baisakhi, Bihu, Vishu, Onam.)

Related to an event of history. (Vijayadashami, Deepawali, Holi.)

Related to a deity. (Krishna—Janmashtami, Rama—Ramanavami, Shiva—Shivaratri, Ganesha—Ganesha Chaturthi, Murugana—Sasthi Vrata, Saraswati—Vasantapanchami, Durga—Durga Puja, Ayyappa—Ayyappa Puja.)

Related to the founder or great personality of a religion. (Buddha—Buddhapaurnima, Nanak—Nanakjayanti, Mahavira—Mahavirajayanti.)

Related to a social custom. (Guru Paurnima, Raksha Bandhan, Bhai Dooj.)

Festival for ladies. (Vatasavitri, Karava Chautha, Chhatha, Kajari Tija, Hartalika, Mangalagaur, Attukal Pongala.)

A special event/occasion. (Snake boat race, festival of kites, Vishwakarma Jayanti, Narada Jayanti.)

Apart from these festivals, there are various pilgrimages-*Yatras* (Char Dham Yatra, Kanvad Yatra, Sabarimala Yatra, Jagannath Rath Yatra, Vaishno Devi Yatra, Amarnath Yatra, Varakari Yatra etc.) and fairs—*Melas* (Kumbha Mela, Ardhakumbha Mela, Ambubachi Mela, fairs on the occasions like Makara Sankranti-Shivaratri-Baisakhi etc.) where a large number of devotees take part with devotion and enthusiasm.

These festivals, pilgrimages and fairs are spread over entire year. (*Some of them are followed in entire Bharat and some are followed in specific regions.*) **Apart from awakening/enhancing spirituality, they beget a feeling of *oneness* in society. Moreover, they release one's burdens related to daily life and thus make a vibrant and joyful atmosphere in society. They are like a *feast* after day-to-day *routine meals* and hence, everyone eagerly awaits them.**

FOUR ASHRAMAS

The life of a human being (taken as 100 years) has been organised into a four-fold division of 25 years each, known as 'Four Ashramas'. They are:

Brahmacharyashrama (0-25), Grihasthashrama (25-50), Vanaprasthashrama (50-75) and

Sanyasashrama (75-100).

It is the result of a well thought over study of human nature and life. ***The first two Ashramas are meant for everyone, whereas the other two Ashramas are optional, but they have been accepted by society as an ideal way to lead one's life and those who opt for them are highly respected.***

Brahmacharyashrama is *bachelorhood/celibacy,* which in a way is *student life,* where the focus is on *discipline, self-restraint, respect for the 'Guru'* [not just a *teacher,* the meaning is 'one who removes ignorance and gives knowledge' {'GU—darkness (representing ignorance)', 'RU—light (representing knowledge)'} or 'dispeller of darkness—inner and outer'] and *devotion towards learning.* It can be seen that most of the student problems which are faced today are due to lack of these virtues. Therefore, these virtues should be inculcated among the students to tackle these problems.

In Brahmacharyashrama, one acquires the knowledge and expertise of essential disciplines needed to earn livelihood and lead a meaningful (*Saarthak*) personal, familial, professional and societal life.

Grihasthashrama is the life of a *householder,* which in a way is *married life,* where the focus is not just on husband, wife and their children; it is on the entire family. For this reason, there are specific names for various relationships in all of our languages (*e.g. in Hindi: Chacha-Chachi, Tau-Taya, Mama-Mami, Mausa-Mausi, Samadhi-Samadhan, Dada-Dadi, Nana-Nani, Bhatija-Bhatiji, Bhanja-Bhanji, Pota-Poti, Nati-Natin, Bua, Jeth, Devar, Bhabhi, Jamai, Bahu, Jija, Sala etc; whereas in English, there are just words like uncle, auntie etc. which are used for several relationships*). These relationships do cover all *'types'* of people that a person comes across in society. Hence, they teach a person how one should behave in society. (That's why, it is said that *'home is the first school to inculcate social behaviour'*.)

Looking at the strong bondage among the family members of a Hindu family, many of the foreign dignitaries (including President, PM of a country) have publicly said that they want to learn and adopt the Hindu family system.

Elsewhere, there is a saying *'The earner will eat'* (Kamanewala Khayega); whereas, in Bharat, the saying is *'Jo Janma Hai Vo Khayega, Kamanewala Khilayega'* (One who is born will eat, the earner will feed). This is possible mainly because of the Grihasthashramis, who take care of not only the non-earning members of their family, but the non-earning members of the society as well. For this reason, it is said that *'Dhanyo Grihasthashrama',* i.e. 'Grihasthashrama is Great'.

Vanaprasthashrama is in a way *retired life,* where one retreats to forest/mountain to lead a life of harmony with nature and for spiritual cause.

Vanaprasthashrama is not mandatory for everyone. One may opt for it or one may not, as per the individual's orientation, aptitude and family condition. The Grihasthashrama continues after the age of 50 for those who do not opt for the Vanaprasthashrama.

In the present-day context, there are two more options for a Vanaprasthi (one who has opted for the Vanaprasthashrama) apart from retreating to forest/mountain: (1) Giving *more time* for social responsibilities while living in home. (2) Leaving home (*but staying in the society, instead of retreating to forest/mountain*) to give *full time* for social/ spiritual responsibilities.

A Vanaprasthi giving more or full time for social/ spiritual responsibilities is useful in two ways:

1. The handing over of family responsibilities to the next generation takes on smoothly. Moreover, the new generation gets the opportunity to run the family at an apt time,

with the availability of experienced persons of family to give suggestions as and when needed (like during a crisis). On the other hand, the old generation encourages the new generation to take up the new responsibility, help them as and when needed (without any interference) and they feel proud about them; which is aptly reflected in the proverb *'Baap Se Beta Sawaai',* i.e. 'Son is better than father'.

2. The society gets benefited due to the experience and expertise of the *Vanaprasthi*, who can find more or full time for social activities, because he/she has been relieved from the family responsibilities.

Sanyasashrama is the life of an *ascetic*—in which all of the worldly ties are renounced to seek ultimate merger with Brahman. It is meant only for a few persons who attain a particular spiritual level and find an apt *Guru* (preceptor/spiritual guide) to give the ascetic initiation (Sanyasa-Diksha). For all other persons, the Vanaprasthashrama (or Grihasthashrama) continues even after the age of 75.

As per the Hindu tradition, the Ashrama system has been flexible and hence, there are many examples where it has not been followed,

e.g. entering Vanaprasthashrama directly from Brahmacharyashrama (many full-time devotees of social and spiritual cause) and entering Sanyasashrama directly from Brahmacharyashrama (Aadi Shankaracharya, Samartha Ramadasa, Swaminarayana, Swami Vivekananda etc.).

SHODASH SANSKAR

The ***'Shodash Sanskar'***[10] (16 sacraments) have been very thoughtfully arrived at to help the body, mind, intellect and soul of everyone to grow in such a way that makes the person an ideal human being. It can be seen that 3 of them fall before birth {*the modern science has also accepted that Sanskaras can be imparted to a human being even before birth and hence, there is an increasing trend of rituals like 'Garbhadhana', 'Punsavana' during pregnancy*}, 7 of them fall before the teenage, 4 of them fall between teenage and 25 years of age, then marriage and finally the last Sanskar of Antyeshti (last rites)—

---

10. There are other descriptions/classifications and regional variations of the 16 Sanskaras. Sometimes, the total number of Sanskaras is taken as other than 16. But, the important thing is—most of the Sanskaras are common and there are Sanskaras during each stage of human life (pre-birth to post-death); with most of them falling during the formative years and hence, they help a person to be an ideal human being.

which is after death. Thus, 14 out of 16 Sanskaras are falling during the formative years of a human being. A truly scientific approach!

The 'Ashram System' and the 'Shodash Sanskaras' need not be followed as they have been in the past. They should be adapted as per current scenario and present-day needs.

MEASUREMENT OF TIME and ALMANAC

The measurement of time (short duration to extremely long duration) has been very precise in Bharat. It has been divided into two categories:

1. Conventional measurement of time (*short to long duration*).

   The smallest unit of conventional time is ***Paramanu*** (approximately equal to 26 micro sec.) and the largest unit is ***Varsha*** (one year, which is equal to 3280500000 Paramanu). There are in all 19 distinct units of measurement of conventional time {Paramanu, Anu, Trasarenu, Truti, ..., Maas (month), Ritu (season—two months), Ayana (half year), Varsha (year)}, with each unit having a specific mathematical relationship with the adjoining units. {100 years are known as "Shat Varsha", 1000 years are known as "Sahasra Varsha" and so on.}

2. Cosmic time measurement (*extremely long duration*).

This starts with the age/era ***Yuga*** which is equal to ***Kaliyuga*** (432000 years). Other eras are: Dwaparayuga, Tretayuga and Satayuga. Then comes Chaturyugi, Manvantara, Kalpa, Brahmaa Varsha and ***Brahmaa Ayu*** (age of Brahmaa—100 Brahmaa Varsha, which is approximately 31 trillion years). These are also precisely inter-related.

The ***'Sankalpa Mantra'***, to be chanted before starting any special worship (*Vishesh Puja*) or religious ceremony (*Anushthan*), includes the terms related to the cosmic time measurements (which are very near to the values given by modern science), like ***Yuga*** (the time taken by all of the planets of our solar system to fall in a straight line), ***Manvantara*** (the time taken by our galaxy '*Milky Way*' to complete one revolution about its own axis), ***Kalpa*** (the time taken by our galaxy to take one round of the next galaxy '*Andromeda*'), ***one day of Brahmaa*** (2 Kalpas), ***life time of the present Universe*** (100 years of Brahmaa), ***age of the present Universe*** (approximately first half of the life time is over) etc. [*These facts have been* *recognised and appreciated by a renowned American cosmologist* ***Carl Sagan*** *in his book 'Cosmos'.*] The Sankalpa Mantra also gives the exact location of the person who is performing the Puja/Anushthan.

[The Sankalpa Mantra: *Adya Brahmane, Dwitiya Parardhe, Shri Shwetavarah Kalpe, Vaivaswat Manvantare, Ashtavinshati Tame Kaliyuge, Pratham Charane, ...*]

The ***Hindu Panchanga*** (almanac) deals with five parts/topics: ***Tithi*** (lunar day), ***Nakshatra*** (Asterisms/a group of stars. 27 in number—Ashwini, Bharani etc.), ***Rashi*** (Zodiac. 12 in number—Mesh, Rishabh etc.), ***Yoga*** (Equal to a lunar day. 27 in number) and ***Karana*** (Half a lunar day. 11 in number, 4 fixed and 7 moveable). These are used for finding out a ***Muhurta*** (auspicious Tithi and time) for marriage, thread ceremony, Bhoomi Poojan (land worship), Griha Pravesh (house warming) etc.; nature and future of a child and a grown-up person based on the birth Tithi and time, and other such things related to Astrology. It's beyond the scope of this book to explain all of these topics in details. However, the *Tithi* and some other things have been explained here briefly.

The *Tithi* (given in the Hindu calendar) is based on the phases of the moon (there are 15 Tithis—

Pratipada, Dwitiya, Ekadashi, Dwadashi, Paurnima, Amavasya etc.). The low and high tides of sea mainly depend on the phases of moon (*they also depend on sun and the spinning/rotation of earth, but both of them have much less effect on the low/high tides of sea than that of phases of moon*), which are given by the corresponding *Tithi,* but the *date* (a solar day, mentioned in other calendars) has nothing to do with the low/high tides of sea. Thus, a *Tithi* has much more in it than a *date*. [The irony is that most of the Hindus don't follow the Hindu calendar in their day-to-day life (*the notable exception is that of Nepal, where the people are following it because their national calendar is Hindu calendar*), although the most important events in their life—the festivals of Holi, Vijayadashami, Deepawali etc; horoscope, marriage, thread ceremony, house warming etc. are based on the Hindu calendar. They even don't know their own *birthTITHI*, albeit they know and celebrate their *birthDAY* !]

Moon is the nearest celestial body in our solar system and the sun is the nearest star. Hence, both of them have a tremendous impact on earth and on the life of a humankind. The Hindu calendar is based on both of them: *Lunar calendar* (based on moon's rotation around earth) and *Solar calendar* (based on earth's rotation around sun). They are the most scientific among all calendars, which is evident in the exactness of the solar and lunar eclipses given in them and other such phenomena occurring in nature.

It's a ***seven-day week*** as in all other calendars. The ***lunar month*** (twelve in a year - Chaitra, Vaishakha etc.) is the period between successive new moons (or full moons) and the ***solar month*** is one twelfths of a tropical year. In Hindu Panchanga, the lunar month is more in use, which consists of two ***Pakshas*** {half of the lunar month - Shukla Paksha (*increasing phases of moon*) and Krishna Paksha (*decreasing phases of moon*)}. There are six ***seasons***[11] {Vasant (spring), Grishma (summer), Varsha (monsoon), Sharad (autumn), Hemant (pre winter) and Shishir (winter)} and two ***Ayanas*** {half of the year—Uttarayana (summer solstice, the sun's northward movement) and Dakshinayana (winter solstice, the sun's southward movement)}.

The Astronomy of Bharat is extremely rich and this is reflected in the near perfect knowledge

---

11. *Perhaps, Bharat is the only major country in the world, where all of these six seasons are existing*—each season lasting for about two months.

about the planets (their size, distance from earth and sun etc.) and stars and Nakshatras (a group of stars) in the sky, which has been recognised by modern science.

VEDAS and SANSKRIT

The ***Vedas*** (Rigveda, Yajurveda, Samaveda and Atharvaveda) are considered as major Hindu treatises. The experts all over the world have accepted that they have been compiled *at least 5000 years ago*[12] and Rigveda is the first book on earth.

The Vedas consist, apart from spirituality, many things related to day-to-day life as well, including science and technology. An organisation *"Vijnana Bharati"* has conducted many International Seminars on the topic *'Science and Technology in Vedas'* (it is to be noted that the topic of the Seminar is not something like *'Spirituality in Vedas'*) where hundreds of research papers have

---

12. (1) The period of Mahabharata has been estimated to be approximately 5000 years ago and there are several references of Vedas in it. (2) The Vedas have several references of river Saraswati in it. (*Therefore, it is believed that they must have been compiled on its banks.*) The archaeological evidences show that the river Saraswati went underground sometime during the *tectonic plate shift* around 4500-5000 years ago.

been presented by the scholars all over the world that are included in their proceedings.

In the World Conference on Ecology (*Earth Summit*) held in Rio de Janeiro (3-14 June 1992), the leader of the Bharatiya delegation Dr Karan Singh distributed the English translation of 63 Shlokas of 'Prithwi-Sukta' from Atharvaveda among all delegates towards the end of the summit. The reaction of many of them was that it should have been distributed on the very first day of the Summit, as it contained several points related to environment protection, which would have been extremely useful during the deliberations.

Swami Bharati Krishna Tirtha (1884-1960) discovered the Vedic Mathematics Sutras (formulae) in Vedas. They consist of 16 Sutras and 13 sub-Sutras, which can be used to carry out various calculations yielding accurate results in a faster and simpler way. Therefore, Vedic maths is gaining popularity all over the world. Several coaching institutes for competitive exams are teaching Vedic maths, so that the students can do fast oral calculations. (*Calculating aids are not allowed in these exams.*) Many great mathematicians of the world have called Vedic maths a magic. Swami Tirtha's reaction to this used to be—it is *magic* if one doesn't know it and *maths* if one knows it.

A few words on Sanskrit : Vedas have been written in Sanskrit and hence it can be said that the antiquity of Sanskrit goes beyond Vedas. It has been accepted by the world's linguistic scholars that Sanskrit is not only the oldest amongst all of the natural languages, it is also the most structured language.

Sanskrit is the only natural language that can serve as an artificial language also. Therefore, it is quite useful in the field of Artificial Intelligence (AI) and many researchers all over the world are working in this direction.

Being a phonetic language, the pronunciation and writing in Sanskrit is perfect and similar everywhere. All of the tongue muscles are utilised while speaking in Sanskrit. (*This is the only language of this kind.*) For this reason, one who is fluent in Sanskrit, can speak in any language (known or unknown) with correct pronunciation. Sanskrit is very useful in *speech therapy* because of this characteristic.

Another uniqueness of Sanskrit is its unchanged form for millennia. The main reason for this is its teaching through *oral tradition*.

Looking into the specialities of Sanskrit (phonetic language, most structured language,

usefulness in the field of computer and AI, speech therapy applications etc.) and the vast treasure of knowledge (spiritual and worldly matters) in Vedas and other treatises, there is a growing trend of Sanskrit studies in Bharat as well as in the entire world. Many of the foreign colleges and Institutes are offering certificate, degree and PG courses and carrying out research work in Sanskrit. There are many Sanskrit Universities in Bharat and other countries. The "*Sanskrit Speaking Classes*" organised by "*Sanskrit Bharati*" are gaining popularity in Bharat and many other countries.

LAW OF ACTION and REBIRTH

Hindu Dharma believes that one has to face the consequences of all of his/her actions/deeds—whether they are *Punya*[13] (can be called a 'noble deed') or *Paap* (sin). No Prophet or Messiah can wash away one's misdeeds. It is to be noted that the consequence for each individual deed is to be faced (and not on the overall nature of all of the deeds put together). This is *Law of Action* (Karma-Siddhanta) and it is in accordance with the '*cause-effect*' theory which is very scientific in nature.

13. It is interesting to note that there is no synonym in English for the word '*Punya*', although for the word '*Paap*', there is a synonym '*Sin*' in it.

The Hindu Dharma believes that one gets *rebirth*[14] (Punarjanma) to face the unfulfilled consequences of his/her deeds in previous births.

The concept of rebirth gives a valid reason for different birth conditions (*in rich family, in poor family; good looking, bad looking; with intellect, mentally retarded etc.*), because the person has not done any deed in the present birth. One understands that it is the consequence of the *baggage of past Karm* (deeds of previous births), both good (Punya) and bad (Paap). On the other hand, the Semitic religions explain this situation as an *'accident of birth'*, which is not a logical explanation, it is just a matter of faith.

Similarly, it also explains as to what will happen to the consequences of the deeds of a person just before death, because the person has no time in the present birth to face the consequences of those deeds. One understands that the consequences will have to be faced during the future births. The Semitic religions explain that the consequences of all of the deeds, including the deeds of a person just before death, will

---

14. The concept of rebirth has been mentioned in almost all of the pre-Christ religions. Negating rebirth has started with the advent of the Semitic religions.

be decided on the *'Day of Judgement'/'Qayamat Ka Din'*, which again is not a logical explanation, just a matter of faith.

It is said that we should not believe in rebirth because we don't remember anything about the previous births. [*In a way, it is good that we don't remember anything about the previous births, because it would have been very confusing and complicated, and hence extremely difficult to live in the present birth, with the memories of the previous births.*] However, just because we don't remember anything about the previous birth, we should not reject the concept of rebirth. We don't remember anything about our infancy, still we accept that stage of our life. It can be said that although we don't remember anything about our infancy, the people we trust do tell us about it and hence, we believe in our infancy stage. We also know that there are a few exceptional persons who do remember about their infancy.

Similarly, there are a few ***Veetaraaga*** (one who is free from the worldly pleasures and attachments) spiritual personalities who do remember about their previous births and they affirm rebirth. Why shouldn't they be believed? Don't we believe in many of the principles of science, although most of us don't know anything about them and their proof? Don't most of us believe in the existence of God, although none of us has seen God? It should always be remembered that ***'absence of proof is not necessarily a proof of absence of happening'***.

The concept of rebirth gives a most logical explanation for (1) different birth conditions and (2) about the consequences of the deeds done just before death. There is no logical explanation to these questions in Semitic religions.

There is one more aspect. **The concept of rebirth *(even if it is assumed to be just a matter of faith)* helps a person in making up his/her mind to accept the adverse situations he/she has to face in life, for which he/she finds no logical explanation because he/she has done nothing wrong of that *magnitude* to have that kind of *punishment*.** A really soothing psychological explanation, very much needed by everyone to accept and carry on with their lives in the given situation without any grudge. Besides this, the concept of rebirth motivates a person to do *Punya* and stay away from *Paap*, so that one can have a better life in the next birth. Isn't it good for society?

The belief in the *Law of Action* should not be misinterpreted as *fatalism* (leaving everything on destiny or fate). The Hindus don't leave everything on destiny and this should be very clearly understood.

There are four types of *Karma*. They are: (1) Prarabdha Karma, (2) Sanchita Karma, (3) Kriyamana Karma and (4) Agami Karma.

The *Prarabdha Karma* is a person's accumulated Karma of all previous lives which has *come to fruition* (begun to bear fruits) in this life. It decides the country and place of birth, parentage, individual conditions of the newly born at the time of birth etc. which can't be changed. One has to accept this and live with it.

The *Sanchita Karma* is the accumulated Karma of all previous lives of a person which has *not yet come to fruition* (yet to begin bearing fruits). It decides the characteristics, nature, tendencies, traits and aptitudes of a person. These can be changed by setting a noble goal in life and making sincere efforts to achieve it, learning from the behaviour of good persons of family and society, reading the biographies of great personalities and other good literature and contemplating on them, determined efforts, regular practice etc. Many such examples can be seen in society.

The *Kriyamana Karma* is the actions of a person in the present life. Some of it will come to fruition later in the present life itself (*Arabdha Karma*), whereas the remaining will come to fruition in the next life (*Anarabdha Karma*). It is well within one's control.

The *Agami Karma* is the future actions of a person in the present life. This also is well within one's control.

Therefore, it can be seen that the effect of Prarabdha Karma (birth place, parentage etc.) is the only predetermined portion of one's life which can't be changed. The effect of Sanchita Karma (characteristics, nature etc.) can be changed by personal efforts and the Kriyamana Karma and Agami Karma are well within one's control. Thus, **in Hindu Dharma, only a meagre is left on destiny, most of the things depend on the deeds in the present life.**

DESIRELESS ACTION

Desireless action (Nishkaama Karma) is an action performed (Kriyamana Karma and Agami Karma) withouth any expectation of fruits or results. Although it helps in getting out of the cycle of birth and death, something more is to be done for that.

There are three types of action. (1) Actions related to daily and compulsory duties (Nitya Karma). (2) Actions related to occasional and obligatory duties. (3) Desire driven actions.

The actions of the first two types do not result in Punya (merit points). However, not discharging the duties or their improper discharge leads to Paap (demerit points).

[An analogy will make this clear. If we drive by following the traffic rules, we don't get *merit points*; but if we break some traffic rules while driving, there is some penalty (*demerit points*).]

There are three types of desire driven action: (1) *Need* (desire to fulfil the essential requirements). No merit or demerit points. (2) *Greed* (desire for the things that are not essential requirements and others have to pay a cost for it). This results in demerit points. (3) *Punya* (can be called as *spiritual merit*) which is (a) a desire for the welfare of others and (b) a desire to know the *ultimate reality*. These result in merit points.

Thus, an individual accumulates a mixed baggage of merit and demerit points during his/her life. If one is successful in performing the desireless action, there won't be any merit or demerit points for the actions of this life.

To be successful in performing the desireless action, one should have a *spiritual mindset*, which is extremely difficult for a human being.

[The way of thinking of a person with '*spiritual mindset*': "The actions are just an offering to the Almighty and my contribution to the collective good", "I am not the doer, the actions are carried out by the Almighty through me", "The actions are not for me, they are for the society and carried out as a duty towards it" and other thoughts on these lines.]

However, even if this is achieved by a person, he/she cannot neutralise the pending baggage of the work done in previous births (Prarabdha Karma and Sanchita Karma). For that, one has to study the scriptures to know and realise the ultimate reality of Brahman. To achieve this, one has to go through three stages:

Shravana (listening, reading and understanding the spiritual Vedic and Upanishadic preaching at intellectual level), *Manana* (contemplate and assimilate them) and *Nididhyaasana* (to attain a direct vision of Brahman through profound and repeated meditation).

These three stages help in neutralising the pending baggage of work done in previous births and then one gets out of the cycle of birth and death.

[There are (and have been) many personalities who do not wish to get out of the cycle of birth and death, instead they pray for rebirths in Bharat, so that they can keep on working for the sake of society and motherland.]

□

3

HINDU SANSKRITI

INTRODUCTION

Every nation has different living conditions (adverse to favourable), economic conditions (very poor to very rich), weather conditions (extreme hot to extreme cold), geographical conditions, different problems, same history, similar beliefs and traditions, specific virtues, values of life etc. They make a philosophy and world view of the people of that nation, which, in turn, creates its ***Sanskriti/Samskriti.***[15]

A major aspect of the Sanskriti of Bharat is that it is based on a philosophy which inculcates the '*spirituality–based view of life*'. Moreover, the world

---

15. *Sanskriti/Samskriti—Sam Kriti.* The similar (*sam*) personal and societal behaviour/actions (*kriti*) of people which is a collective outcome of same ancestors, history, traditions, music-art-literature, values of life, thought process and conduct in its light, goals of life etc. In short, it is *the way of life of the people of a nation.*

view of Bharat is also spiritual.

Bharat is known as Hindustan, because of the Hindus who have been living here since ages. Therefore, the Sanskriti of Bharat is known as **Hindu Sanskriti**. [Other names are *Bharatiya Sanskriti* and *Indian culture*. The later one is named after India, another name for Bharat. Culture is taken as the English word for Sanskriti, which is not an exact synonym. (*More on this at a later stage in this chapter.*) However, the meaning of all of the three is the same.]

The society of Bharat has always been *Dharma follower* and hence, all of the virtues and values of life associated with Dharma (*which have been discussed earlier*) are naturally incorporated in Hindu Sanskriti. Moreover, the living conditions in Bharat are such (*Sujalam, Sufalam,* ...... as described in '*Vande Mataram*') that one can lead a calm and peaceful life and hence, one can actually be *Bha-Rat* (*Bha*: light, which symbolises knowledge, *Rat*: engrossed; i.e. engrossed in the pursuit of knowledge). **This precisely is the reason as to why Bharat could conceive the wonderful concept of *Dharma*.**

PRAKRITI, SANSKRITI and VIKRITI

There are three distinct words in Sanskrit—

Prakriti *(natural tendency),* ***Sanskriti*** and ***Vikriti*** *(perversion).* The entire animate world (except the human beings) leads life as per its *Prakriti* (Prakriti Dharma), i.e. its natural tendency, as given by the Almighty. On the other hand, a human being can lead the life beyond its *Prakriti,* because of the mind and intellect. *(It can be said that the Almighty has* 'programmed' *the lives of every creature other than the human beings and hence, they lead their entire life as per this* 'program'; *whereas the human beings are left* 'non-programmed' *by the Almighty and hence, they can lead their life as per their wish because of their mind and intellect.)* When it goes in forward direction (upgradation), it is *Sanskriti* and when it goes in backward direction (degradation), it is *Vikriti.*

For example, to eat food is Prakriti, to give one's food to others is Sanskriti and to snatch others' food is Vikriti. {*Prakriti can be taken as something like a zero in Mathematics. When someone goes on the right side of zero (forward direction), the number is positive (Sanskriti) and when someone goes on the left side of zero (backward direction), the number is negative (Vikriti).*} Only human beings have the capability of going to Sanskriti or Vikriti. Rest of the entire animate world is always confined to its Prakriti.

It is the human society that decides as to which is the forward/positive direction (leading to Sanskriti) and which is the backward/negative direction (leading to Vikriti). The Sanskritis of nations are different, because the people of each nation have a typical mindset due to several reasons (*given at the beginning of this chapter*) and hence, their conception of positive and negative directions need not be the same.

The virtues that take a human being towards ***Sanskriti*** are to be inculcated in him/her through ***Sanskaras*** (which make a human being virtuous and remove one's bad qualities). Other human beings (mother, father, Guru, great personalities, wise and elderly people etc.), good books, devotional songs, music-art-literature, places of worship (Mandir-Mutth-Gurudwara) and education (Ashrama-Gurukul-School-College) and the environment (of village/town/city/province/country) are capable of imparting Sanskaras.

The environment of Sanskaras prevails in society due to a large number of individuals who are *Sanskarit* (having good Sanskaras). This is known as *Sanskriti* of the society. Thus, ***Sanskaras are of the individuals and Sanskriti is of the society.***

SANSKARAS and BRAIN-WASHING

Sometimes, it may appear that Sanskaras are like

brain-washing. Therefore, the difference between the two should be very clearly understood.

Imparting 'Sanskaras' is bringing up a progeny by moulding its mind in such a way that it makes him/her an ideal citizen. They are *imparted* by someone who is very close and respected (e.g. mother, father, Guru). He/she teaches about what is good, what is bad; what should be done, what should not be done etc., and leaves it to the discretion of the individual to accept (either immediately or slowly) or reject. Thus, it is the individual who takes the decision, there is no compulsion whatsoever. On the other hand, **in *brain-washing,* the *brain* is supposed to be contaminated and hence, it needs *washing,* which is done by someone who is mostly unknown till then, and in a way, the brain is *forced* to accept whatever is being told.**

A *Sanskarit person* is always useful to society because of his/her virtues. On the other hand, the thinking process of a *brain-washed person* is heavily one sided, he/she lacks discretion and hence, is like a stooge in the hands of the one who has brain-washed the person who may exploit him/her in many inhuman acts of fanaticism and terrorism. Therefore, a brain-washed person is usually a threat to society.

Following are the main differences between

imbibing Sanskaras (*Sanskar Grahan-SG*) and *Brain-Washing-BW:*

- SG is *from within* (innermost control), BW is *controlled by others* (remote control).
- In SG, the *role of discretion is pivotal*, in BW *it is negligible.*
- In SG, the actions are decided by an *individual*, in BW they are decided by *others.*
- In SG, the individual is considered as a *practitioner* (Sadhak), in BW he/she is considered as a *tool.*
- SG is *natural*, BW is *artificial.*

EQUAL RESPECT FOR ALL RELIGIONS

The Hindu Sanskriti has a special feature of *having equal respect for all religions* (Samaadara). Because of this, Bharat has always given refuge to the people who were driven out of their own country by the invaders or by the intolerant fanatic people of their society. All of them were given a warm welcome and all facilities were provided to them to follow their religion, including the construction of their places of prayer and worship. *Parsis* (Zoroastrians, who came from Iran) and *Yahudis* (Jews, who came from Israel) of Bharat are the living evidence. Thus, it can be seen that there has always been ***'Spiritual Democracy'*** (each religion having equal right/opportunity to be followed and grow without any discrimination—either by the society or by the rulers) in Bharat.

The welcome treatment was also extended to the persons who came as friendly explorers or visitors. So far as the invaders like Greek, Shaka, Hoona, Kushana, Arab, Turk, Mughal, Pathan etc. are concerned, they came as an enemy (EITHER to Loot OR to Loot and rule OR to Loot, rule and convert) and got the treatment accordingly. The Europeans like British, Portuguese, French, Dutch etc. who came as traders, were given the welcome treatment initially. However, later on they began to behave like an enemy by trying to establish their rule and convert the people by force or by hook and crook. Therefore, they also got the treatment given to an enemy. *This entire period is a very inspring chapter of history of Bharat.*

ATITHI DEVO BHAVA

In earlier days, there were no hotels or restaurants and hence, the travellers and pilgrims, who were mostly pedestrians, used to go to the homes enroute to take shelter, rest, medical help, water, food or for any other help. It has been a tradition in Bharat to treat such people sympathetically, instead of avoiding or misbehaving with them, even though they were unknown and had arrived unannounced (A-tithi). The highest degree of respect was to treat them like God (Atithi Devo Bhava).

[In the present-day context, the feeling of 'Atithi Devo Bhava' can be expressed by constructing free of charge guest house (Dharmashala) and places to rest in the shadow of trees and other convenient places, free medical help, arrangement of free food and drinking water (Annadana and Pyau) etc. Thus, the *personal* feeling of 'Atithi Devo Bhava' can have its *social* transformation.]

WELL-BEING OF THE ENTIRE UNIVERSE

The Hindu Sanskriti has a special feature of wishing the well-being of *ALL* human beings (not just Hindus), aptly reflected in the prayer ***'Sarve Bhavantu Sukhinah'*** (may everyone be happy). It should be noted that it's not '***Hindave** Bhavantu Sukhinah*'. Similar feelings are expressed in the sayings '***Bhavatu Sabba Mangalam***' (may there be well-being of everyone) and '***Sarbat Da Bhala***' (welfare of all). Wishing well-being of *ALL* has also been extended to the entire animate-inanimate world and universe, which is reflected in another prayer ***'Aum Dyou Shantih, Antarikshah Shantih, Prithivi Shantih, Aapah Shantih, Oshadhayah Shantih, Vanaspatayah Shantih,......'***.

The desire for the well-being of the entire universe is not confined only to the prayers and treatises. They have been reflected in the day-to-day life of Hindus in the form of certain traditions. (*Practical implementation of 'Atithi Devo Bhava', the importance given to the service of deprived people, to give first Roti to a cow and last to a dog, to feed wheat flour to ants and insects, to feed eatables to fishes-animals-birds, to keep water for animals and birds, taking care of environment, harvesting the natural resources rather than exploitation of nature, ...*) In one of the folk songs sung by the peasant women folk, they pray to God that let there be a bumper crop so that it can be given to the monks, Atithis, needy people, animals, birds, insects etc, and also to the family members. (*It should be noted that* 'family members' *have been mentioned as* "also" *and it appears after the monks, Atithis etc. in the song.*)

EDUCATION SYSTEM

In earlier days, the *education system* was *Gurukul*-based. (The student—known as *Shishya*—used to reside in the *Ashrama* of a Guru for education.) They used to go to the nearby houses for *Bhiksha* (*alms*, which is not *begging*). The householders (mostly ladies) used to give them plenty of *Bhiksha*—treating them with affection and respect, not like a beggar. In this way, the society was supporting the then prevailing education system; apart from donating various things to the *Ashramas*.

[In the present-day context, the society can support the education system by way of giving private scholarship, prize, sponsorship for higher education, free coaching, bearing the expenses of poor and underprivileged students, adopting a private school (*full or a part of it*), commencing private education trust/society and other such means.]

INDEBTEDNESS

The feeling of indebtedness (Kritajnata) is one of the major features of Hindu Sanskriti.

There are three basic debts on a human being, namely:

1. ***Rishi Rin*** (debt of the sages)—To get indebted, one has to study and understand the spiritual and other good literature, and teach it to others. (This is *Brahma Yajna*.)
2. ***Pitri Rin*** (debt of the ancestors)—To get indebted, one has to pray in a specific way (*Shraaddha*) for the *Mukti* of the ancestors, particularly during the Pitripaksha—the Krishnapaksha of Ashwin. (*This is Pitri Yajna*.)

3. ***Deva Rin*** (debt of God)—To get indebted, one has to perform three *Yajnas*.
   a. ***Deva Yajna***: To adore and worship God.
   b. ***Bhoota Yajna***: To take care of animals, birds and insects by giving water and eatables to them.
   c. ***Nru Yajna***: To do useful social work in society for the welfare of others. This is one of the ways of serving God. [Swami Vivekananda has said—"*Nara Sewa Narayana Sewa*". (Serving a human being is serving a God.)]

Apart from getting indebted from all of the above three basic debts, one also feels indebted towards the persons who have done something for him/her and tries to do something in return. Thus, the Kritajnata goes much beyond saying just '*Thank you*' and then forgetting everything. It inculcates the feeling of doing something for the people who have done something for him/her.

[There is a custom in Bharat which is followed everywhere. When someone gives something in a pot to someone, then while returning it, something is always kept inside it as a token of gratitude (*the pot is never returned empty*).]

The feeling of indebtedness is extended towards the animals, plants and trees which are useful to us (like Cow, Tulsi, Peepal and Banyan tree) and they are bowed down to and worshipped. (Cow and Tulsi are considered as mother, and Peepal and Banyan trees are worshipped.)

The feeling of indebtedness is extended even towards the inanimate things as well, which are useful to us; like rivers, mountains, vehicles, various tools and instruments, weapons, stages, playgrounds etc. (River is considered as *Lokamata*—the mother of people, weapons and vehicles are worshipped on Vijayadashami, tools and instruments are worshipped on Vishwakarma Jayanti, and stage and playgrounds are bowed down to.)

HINDU PHILOSOPHY and ITS INFLUENCE

The Western philosophy (which is materialistic) believes in the principles of ***'Survival of the fittest'*** and ***'Matsya Nyaya'*** (the big fish eats the small fish). On the other hand, the Hindu philosophy (which is based on Dharma and hence there is a proper balance between materialism and spirituality in it) believes in ***'Survival of the weakest'*** and ensures it. It also says that the ***'Matsya Nyaya'*** is not applicable to human beings, it is the ***'Manav Nyaya'*** (the strong human beings will protect the weak human beings) which is applicable to them.

The Western philosophy, under the influence of the present-day concept of ***globalisation***, says that ***'the world is a market'*** and hence, everyone is treated as a ***consumer***, who is to be ***exploited*** for more and more profit. (In the earlier days, others were looked at by them as someone who is to be ***conquered.***)

On the other hand, the Hindu world view believes in ***'Vasudhaiva Kutumbakam'*** (the entire world is a family) and ***'Swadesho Bhuvanatrayam'*** (Bhuvanatrayam—earth, heaven and hell—i.e. the entire world—is like one's own country). Hence, everyone is treated as a ***family member*** and a ***fellow country person***.

This is the basic reason as to why other countries became, and are trying to become, a ***Vishwavijeta*** (*conqueror* of the world)—on military ground in earlier days and presently on economic ground. On the other hand, Bharat had been and would be a ***Vishwaguru*** (*preceptor* of the world).

The ancient signs of Vishwaguru can be seen all over the world, not only in several visible forms, but also in the form of influence of Hindu philosophy and world view over the Pre-Christ world. This is the main reason for the Pre-Christ religions to have many similarities with Hindu Dharma.

Many of the earlier philosophers, scientists, writers and other intellectuals of the world (*Arthur Schopenhauer, Albert Einstein, Ervin Schrodinger, Werner Heisenberg, T. S. Eliot, H. G. Wells, Bernard Shaw, Annie Besant, Romain Rolland, Julius R. Oppenheimer, Niels Bohr, Mark Twain, Leo Tolstoy, Arnold Toynbee, Hu Shih, Barbara S. Miller, Carl Sagan et al*) had been influenced by the Hindu philosophy and world view.

The present-day thinkers of the world (*Fritjof Capra, Al Gore, Barack Obama, Linda Johnson, Maria Wirth, Claude Arpi, Arthur Versluis, Brian D. Josephson, Jack Sarfatti, Paul William Roberts, Rick Briggs, David Osborn, Georges Ifrah et al*) are concerned about the grave problems the world is facing today and most of them have realised that the solution lies in the Hindu philosophy and world view.

The effect of getting influenced earlier and the present-day realisation can be seen in the Western world. Some such examples are given below:

(1) Racism, slavery and apartheid have been rejected by them. They are now accepting not only the human rights but the rights of the animate world and inanimate world (like rivers, mountains etc.) as well.

(2) Gradual acceptance of the integrated/ comprehensive/holistic approach (as per Hindu philosophy) instead of the fragmented/ reductionist/piecemeal approach (as per Western philosophy).

(3) Gradual change in the mindset of people from 'exploitation of nature' to 'harvesting the natural resources'.

The worldwide acceptance of *Yoga* is another example of this sort. {The United Nations resolution of the *International Yoga Day on every 21st June* (the date of longest day and shortest night in the Northern Hemisphere where 90% of world population lives - the summer solstice) has been supported by almost all countries in the year 2015, because of their realisation that Yoga is extremely useful for health and peace of mind. Since then, this day is being celebrated all over the world every year with great fervour and enthusiasm, where apart from the Bharatiyas, a large number of natives are also taking part in it.} There are many more features of Hindu Sanskriti which are attracting the world today. {e.g. *Hindu philosophy professed in the treatises Veda, Upanishada, Bhagavad Gita, Aagam, Tripitak, Guru Granth Sahib; Bharatiya classical music and dance; Sanskrit, Ayurveda etc.*}

The *spirit of service* (Sewabhava) has been seen and appreciated by the entire world during the world wide Covid-19 pandemic, when thousands of common people at every place have helped lacs of needy persons, in addition to the help provided by the Central and State Governments. The Hindu family system has captured the imagination of the entire world and as mentioned earlier in this book, they want to learn and adopt it. Moreover, Bharat can show the world a ***path of sustainable development***[16] based on the principle of ***'progress - based on coordination'***, which is eco-friendly and with human face. All of this would take Bharat to the status of *Vishwaguru*.

Bharat has followed this path of sustainable development successfully for thousands of years and has been at the helm of the world in all respects (*from material wealth to spiritual wealth*). This is

---

16. As per the philosophy behind this path, a humankind is composed of four hierarchically organised attributes of body, mind, intellect and soul; not just a body. Therefore, apart from consideration for the happiness of the body; it takes care of the happiness of mind, intellect and soul as well. Moreover, it believes in oneness of all of the four entities : individual, society, creation and Almighty. For this reason, there is coordination among them everywhere, all the time; rather than having conflicts. Hence, a sustainable development can be achieved by following this path.

known as the ***'Third Way'*** because *Capitalism* is considered as the ***'First Way'*** of development and *Communism* as the ***'Second Way'***. (Both of them are based on the principle of ***'progress - based on conflict'***.) Capitalism is just a few centuries old and is on the verge of failure, whereas Communism is only a century old and has already failed. Therefore, the thinkers of the world are taking keen interest in the path of sustainable development of Bharat, which they called as the ***'Third Way'***. However, it should be called as the ***First Way***; because it is thousands of years old, whereas the other two paths are just a few centuries old or even less than that. Therefore, they should be called as the ***Second Way*** and the ***Third Way***.

SOME FEATURES OF HINDU SANSKRITI

In Hindu Sanskriti, the emphasis is on ***'Tyaga'*** (sacrifice) rather than on ***'Bhoga'*** (enjoyment/ rejoice). **[***So far as rejoice is concerned, the saying is* ***'Tena Tyakten Bhunjeethaah'*** *(rejoice by giving away).* For this reason, one tries to fulfil only the *needs* (rather than being driven by *greed*) with an effort to minimise them, so that one can give more to others.**]**

Therefore, one has a tendency to think about

others before thinking for oneself, which results in a good relationship with everyone and hence a harmonious atmosphere prevails in the society. Moreover, this also ensures the well-being of the under privileged people of society, because he/she works for their betterment due to his/her sacrificing nature. **The Saffron colour, which symbolises sacrifice (apart from valour and piety), commands highest respect in society and one of the common virtues of all of the persons who are considered as great personalities is that all of them have done everything or most of the things for the sake of society and nation.** On the contrary, the persons who have done nothing or very little for the sake of society and nation are never considered as great personalities, even if they are mighty kings or very rich/ intelligent persons.

Another meaning of *Tyaga* is renunciation. In Hindu Sanskriti, it is said that one should renounce *egotism* and the *desire to have fruits of action (Karmafala).* Sometimes, the second one is misunderstood as the 'renouncement of action', which is not possible, because no living person can renounce action. It is the 'desire to have fruits of action' which is to be renounced.

Whenever there is a conflict of interest among

any two entities (Dharma-Sankat) and a question comes up as to which one should be renounced, the Hindu Sanskriti says that the interest of the bigger entity should be taken care of and the smaller entity should be renounced. This has been explained in the following *Shloka*:

Tyajet Ekam Kulasyarthe
Gramasyarthe Kulam Tyajet
Gramam Janapadasyarthe
Atmarthe Prithivim Tyajet

[Renounce an individual for the sake of family, the family for the sake of village, the village for the sake of district and the entire earth for the sake of divine knowledge {Atma → Atmajnana → Brahmajnana (divine knowledge)}.]

In Hindu Sanskriti, the emphasis is on ***'Duty'*** rather than on ***'Right'***. This ensures the protection of the rights of others and helps in maintaining harmony in the society. If the emphasis is on *'Right'* rather than on *'Duty'*, there will be various types of conflicts in the society. (It should not be misunderstood that there is no consideration for individual rights in Hindu Sanskriti. It is the emphasis on Duty, which takes care of the individual rights of everyone.)

The Hindu Sanskriti believes that ***husband and wife are not just equal, they complement (Parasparapuraka) each other.*** One is incomplete without the other. The principle of *complementing each other* is applicable to *man and woman* as well. This has been symbolically expressed in one of the forms of Shiva—the *ArdhaNaariNateshwara*—depicted as half male and half female. This principle is applicable not only to husband-wife and man-woman, it is also applicable to *any two persons.*

The Hindu Sanskriti not only believes in complementing each other, it also believes in interdependence (Parasparavalambana) and a tendency to follow each other (Parasparanukarana). **[***With the advent and acceptance of the theory of relativity and quantum mechanics, the Western world has now started accepting the Universality of above beliefs at philosophical level and* (to some extent) *practical level.***]**

In Hindu Sanskriti, the best possible way of giving respect is to consider someone as mother. For this reason, the cow, rivers, plant Tulsi etc. are considered as mother. Even, the male deity Vitthala/Vithu (the reincarnation of Krishna) is addressed as *Vithu Mauli* (mother Vithu) and Sant Gyaneshwar is addressed as *Gyaneshwar Mauli.*

A woman is known as '*Ramu Ki Ma*' (mother of Ramu) or '*Radha Ki Ma*' (mother of Radha), rather than as '*Mrs so and so*'. Any woman other than one's wife is considered as a mother. (*Matrivat Paradareshu.*)[17] **If this Hindu view to look at women is propagated and followed in society, there will be minimum crimes against them, because the main reason for such crimes is objectification of women.**

TRUTH

The Hindu Sanskriti is a staunch believer of 'truth'. **[*Hindutva is a continuous exploration of truth—***

---

17. After a victory in one of the battles against a Muslim ruler, Chhatrapati Shivaji's solders brought for him the beautiful daughter in law of the defeated ruler of Kalyan (*because the Muslim rulers used to do the same thing with the women of the defeated Hindus*). But Shivaji, being a true Hindu, treated her as a motherly figure and said to her—"*I too would have been handsome, if my mother was as beautiful as you*" and respectfully sent her back to her home and issued a strict order afterwards not to treat women like this (*even if they are Muslims*) and to give them utmost respect.

    Swami Vivekananda was a very handsome youth. During his America visit, a beautiful young American lady got attracted to him and urged that she wants a son like him (*she meant that she wants to marry him and have a son like him*). The immediate response of Swami Vivekananda to this was—"I am your son, please be my mother".

Mahatma Gandhi.] Two of the very popular phrases all over Bharat are ***'Satyameva Jayate'*** (truth alone triumphs) and ***'Satyam Vada, Dharmam Chara'*** (speak the truth and abide by Dharma).

There are two levels of truth. (1) The absolute/supreme level of truth/reality (*Paraa*—transcendental truth/reality, the Paarmaarthik Satya). This corresponds to philosophy. (2) The lower level of truth (*Aparaa*—empirical truth/reality, the Vyaavahaarik Satya). This corresponds to day-to-day life and religion.

A human mind can comprehend only a partial truth. Moreover, **a truth has several facets and for this reason, many of our ancestors (including several sages), have tried to know these facets and none of them have ever been labelled as *non-believers* and persecuted, even when their observations/conclusions were against the then prevailing religions and the popular and accepted beliefs of the society.** On the contrary, some of them have been considered as a Rishi (e.g. Kanada) or a Philosopher (e.g. Charvaka—the first exponent of '*Materialism*'). But in Semitic religions, such people have been condemned, their works have been banned and destroyed and they have been tortured, jailed and even killed—labelling them as a *non-believer* and *heretic* (e.g. Bruno, Copernicus, Galileo, Abdullah Bin Khatal, Mollah Lutfi etc.)

MULTIPLE IDENTITIES

Every individual and group has a desire to preserve its *identity* and wants its continuance. This is very natural and there is absolutely no problem in it. However, when *egotism* comes in, the feeling of superiority and inferiority also comes along with it and then here are several problems and conflicts. (*'I am superior to others', 'my language/caste/religion is superior to other languages/castes/religions' and other thoughts like this.*)

In Hindu philosophy, there is a concept of a *super identity* and every identity is linked with it and is subservient to it. This ensures that egotism does not crop up along with identity. [*An individual has a super identity of his family, a family has a super identity of caste/village/city and a caste/village/city has a super identity of nation.* (Maharshi Aurobindo has said—"Presently, there is no bigger identity than nation, which is an organic and live identity like it.") *Thus, there are multiple identities and everyone is proud of all of them.***]** In this way, every identity is preserved and at the same time, there is no question of egotism and the problems and conflicts that follow it.

HONESTY

How the Hindu Sanskriti and Western culture look at the virtue *Honesty* (Pramanikata) can be clearly understood by following phrases:

*"Pramanikata Yaha **Jeevana Nishtha** Hai"* (*Honesty is the **faith and basic tenet of life***) in Hindu Sanskriti. [Therefore, a person is always honest, whether it is to his/her advantage or disadvantage.]

*"Honesty is the **best policy**"* in Western culture. [Therefore, a person is honest only when it is to his/her advantage.]

KNOWLEDGE

A peculiarity of Hindu Sanskriti is that *knowledge* is considered as a *purifier* and one which helps in achieving *Mukti (spiritual liberation)*— as has been mentioned in the phrase *"**Saa Vidya Yaa Vimuktaye**"* (knowledge is that which liberates).

How knowledge leads one to happiness has been nicely explained in the following Shloka:

Vidya Dadati Vinayam
Vinayad Yati Patratam
Patratwat Dhanamapnoti
Dhanat Dharmam Tatah Sukham

Knowledge (Vidya) yields courtesy (Vinaya), courtesy yields worthiness (Patrata), worthiness yields wealth (Dhana) and wealth yields Dharma and happiness (Sukha).

Thus, there is a spiritual and Dharmik angle to knowledge. This motivates one to share his/her knowledge with others. For this reason, *Bharat has always shared the knowledge with the world, without expecting anything in return.*

[There had been several Universities (*in true sense*) in Bharat, which had been functioning for many centuries. They were open to the entire world for knowledge seekers and a large number of them were educated from these Universities.

Some of these ancient Universities are—

1. Takshashila in today's Pakistan (5th century BCE)
2. Sharada Peeth Temple University in Kashmir (4th century BCE)
3. Pushpagiri in Odisha (2nd century BCE)
4. Nagarjunakonda in Andhra (2nd century CE)
5. Telhara in Bihar (3rd century CE)

6. Nalanda in Bihar (5th century CE)
7. Vallabhi in Gujrat (5th century CE)
8. Vikramshila in Bihar (8th century CE)
9. Morena Golden Triangle University in MP (8th century CE)
10. Somapura in today's Bangla Desh (9th century CE)
11. Kanthalloor Sala University in TN (9th century CE)
12. Jagaddala in today's Bangla Desh (11th century CE)
13. Nadia in Bengal (12th century CE)]

In Western philosophy, knowledge is considered as a *power* and hence, it is used as a weapon to establish one's superiority over others. One never wants to share it with others. (The concept of *patent* is the outcome of this mindset.) Therefore, the path of knowledge to happiness in the Western world is :

Knowledge → conceit (in place of courtesy because it is considered as a power) and worthiness → wealth → happiness (Dharma is absent and hence one enjoys the superiority over others).

OPEN-MINDEDNESS

The Hindu Sanskriti teaches one to be open-minded towards all thoughts, aptly reflected in one of the sayings ***"Aa No Bhadraah Kratavo Yantu Vishwatah"*** (let noble thoughts come to us from entire world). This is one of the reasons as to why the Hindus have a mindset of welcoming all of the thoughts (whether they belong to religious beliefs or worldly matters) and their accommodative and assimilative nature.

INWARD-LOOKING APPROACH

The Hindus believe in ***"Yat Pinde Tat Brahmaande"*** (whatever is in the humankind, the same is in the Universe). A corollary to this belief is—"*If one wants to know about the Universe, first of all he/she must fully understand himself/herself.*" For this reason, the approach of the Hindus is usually *inward-looking* (Antarmukhi) rather than being *outward-looking* (Bahirmukhi).

The inward-looking approach helps in realising (1) one's own mistakes/lacunas and making necessary amends and (2) the goal of life and the duties to be performed to achieve it. However, the inner-outer purity of body, mind and intellect is essential for this.

POSITIVE MINDSET

The Hindu Sanskriti begets a positive mindset in

a person. This can be seen in following traditions:

1. When someone is bidding farewell, it is never said that '*Mein Jaa Raha/Rahi Hoon*' (I am *going*), it is always said that '*Main Aa Raha/Rahi Hoon*' (I am *coming*). The reason is very simple—*going* is considered as bad (negative connotation) while *coming* is considered as good (positive connotation).
2. While closing a shop, it is never said that '*Main Dukan Band Kar Raha/Rahi Hoon*' (I am *closing* the shop), it is always said that '*Main Dukan Badha Raha/Rahi Hoon*' (I am *extending* the shop). The reason is—*closing* is considered as bad (negative connotation) while *extending* is considered as good (positive connotation).
3. When someone is using bad words for a person, it is said that "*Vah Mujhe Bhala-Bura Kah Raha/Rahi Hai*". The literary meaning of this sentence is "He/she is using *good and bad* words for me", but the implied meaning is "He/she is using *bad* words for me".
4. When one is worried about someone that something bad might have happened to him/her, it is always said that "*Uska Koi Bhala-Bura To Nahin Hua Hoga?*" (Has something

good or bad happened to him/her?"), rather than saying *"Uska Koi Bura To Nahin Hua Hoga?"* (Has something *bad* happened to him/her?").

There are many such examples of saying one thing but meaning something else. This shows the positive way of thinking even in day-to-day life, and therefore, one always thinks about positive things rather than negative ones. A wonderful example of *positive mindset*!

UNIQUE FEATURES OF HINDU SANSKRITI

The unique traditions of ***Ghaluwa*** (to give little more to the buyer than the measure/weight) and ***Bohni*** (the first selling of the day by the seller) are being followed everywhere in Bharat and there are specific words for them in all of the Bharatiya languages.

The first one (Ghaluwa) is *in favour of the buyer*. It is sort of a *gesture by the seller* to compensate for any possible mistake of giving less than the desired measure/weight (an Adharma), even if it had been done unknowingly. [This is due to the *'Dharma Bhiru'* (the meaning is not *'one who is afraid of Dharma'*, it is *'one who is very conscious that none of his conduct is against the Dharma'*) nature of Hindus.]

The second one (Bohni) is *in favour of the seller*. When a buyer is not agreeing to the price mentioned by the seller, usually he/she starts bargaining. However, if the seller says "sir/madam, it is my *Bohni*", the buyer immediately stops bargaining and accepts the price mentioned by the seller. This is sort of a *goodwill gesture by the buyer*—a way to say *good luck for the day's selling* to the seller. [This is due to the typical mindset of Hindus, which believes in the principles of '*live and let live*' and '*well-being of ALL*'.]

In Hindu Sanskriti, the donation for a noble cause is always given in the form of ***'Ekadhika'*** (additional one) like 101, 501, 1001; it is never given in round figures like 100, 500, 1000. The reason is: 100, 500, 1000 ...... signify end (it means—no future donations), and hence, it is like a full stop; whereas, 101, 501, 1001 ...... signify continuance (it means—the donations will be given in future also), and hence, it is like a comma.

NAMING OF THE CHILD

The Hindu children are named after the Gods and Goddesses as well (Rama, Krishna, Shankara, Seeta, Laxmi, Saraswati etc.) apart from other names. On the other hand, in Semitic religions, children are never named as Yahweh, Jehovah, Adonai, Elohim, Allah etc.

The reason is—Hindus believe in *'Nara Se Narayana'* (a human being can become a God/Goddess because of his/her noble deeds) and hence, such names are given to children; whereas in Semitic religions, it is said that *'forget about being a God, one can't even* see *a God'*, and hence, no such names are given to children.

REFERRING TO A DECEASED PERSON

After the death of a Hindu, the person is referred to as *Swargavasi* (Swa. Sh/Ss ......) *or Kailasavasi* (Kai. Sh/Ss......) *or Vaikunthavasi* (Vai. Sh/Ss...) because it is believed that the soul of the person may reach Swarga or Kailasa or Vaikuntha because of his/her noble deeds. (*Swarga* is the abode of Indra, *Kailasa* is the abode of Shiva and *Vaikuntha* is the abode of Vishnu.)

On the other hand, such things are never said about a deceased person in Semitic religions; because the person has to wait in the grave till the *'Day of Judgement'* or '*Qayamat Ka Din*' for his/her fate to be decided. Therefore, simply it is said that the person has died (Late Mr./Ms. ......).

[The condolence message *'RIP'* (Rest In Peace) is meant only for a Semitic person, who has to wait in the grave till his/her fate is decided. For a Hindu, it should be something like *'May God bestow Sadgati (liberation) to the departed soul'*.**]**

PROVERBS-IDIOMS and GAMES

Some of the beliefs and principles of Hindu Sanskriti are being reflected in some of the ***Proverbs-Idioms*** and they appear in all of the Bharatiya languages with similar meaning. For example,

DHARMA, ADHARMA—***'Parahitasarasa Dharam Nahin Bhai, Parapeedasam Nahin Adhamai'*** (welfare of others is Dharma, giving pain to others is Adharma).

LAW OF ACTION—***'Jaisi Karani Vaisi Bharani'*** (as is the deed, so is the result), ***'Kar Bhala To Ho Bhala, Kar Bura To Ho Bura'*** (good deeds deliver good result, bad deeds deliver bad result).

TRUTH—***'Saanch Baraabar Tap Nahin, Jhooth Baraabar Paap'*** (there is no penance like a truth and sin like a lie), ***'Jhooth Ke Paon Kahaan'*** (a lie has no legs—*hence it is always caught, because it can't run away*).

CHARITY—***'Ek Haath De To Doosare Ko Pata Na Chale'*** (when one hand gives, the other should not know—*charity should be without any propaganda*).

KNOWLEDGE—***'Jati Na Poochho Sadhu Ki, Poochha Leejo Jnan'*** (do not look at the caste of a noble person, look at his knowledge).

CONTENTMENT—***'Santosh Dhana Hee Param***

Dhana' (a contented mind is real wealth), ***'Laalach Buri Balaa'*** (greed is a big curse).

COURTESY—***'Phaladaar Vriksha Ki Daal Neeche Jhukati Hai'*** (the branch of a tree with ample fruits bends down).

In the same way, there is a reflection of some of the beliefs and principles of Hindu Sanskriti in some of the ***Indigenous Games.*** For example,

The belief in REBIRTH is reflected in the games of ***Kabaddi*** and ***Chess.***

The effect of VIRTUES and VICES on our life is indirectly mentioned in the game of ***Snakes and Ladders***. (The ***virtues***—mentioned in the corresponding square along with the number—take one to a ***ladder*** for ascend in life whereas the ***vices***—mentioned in the corresponding square along with the number—result in one's downfall through ***snake***.)

The PARAM DHAAM—MOKSHA is the name given to the winning position in several games. (*It signifies the ultimate goal of human life.*)

CONVERSION and ASSIMILATION

There are some pairs of words which outwardly look similar, but their meanings are different. Therefore, there should be proper understanding of their meanings. Such pairs will be dealt with in the remaining sections of this chapter. One of such pairs is Conversion-Assimilation.

Although conversion and assimilation (Atmasatikarana) have two sides (first side and other side), there is a basic difference between the two.

In conversion, the first side believes that the religion and culture of the other side is totally inapt and hence in their opinion, either their religion and culture are to be changed by using all possible means or they are to be annihilated. When the first side is successful, they are the winners and the existence—religious and cultural identity—of the other side vanishes completely. There is only the first side. [This has happened all over the world, which has been described in one of the famous Urdu poetry (Shaayari)—"*Yoonaana (Greece), Misra (Egypt), Romaan (Italy) Sab Mit Gaye Jahaan Se*". It means that the original religious and cultural identity of these countries has vanished completely and now they are following different religions and cultures. {Although, the poet (Shaayar) has mentioned only about three countries, there are many more such countries in the world.}] Thus, *conversion is demonic.*

In assimilation, the other side is viewed by

the first side with a mindset of recognition and mutual exchange; and hence, their behaviour towards them is that of equality and sincerity. Therefore, there is no question of a winner or a loser and in the end, both sides voluntarily become one, without any force, each side learning good things from the other side (mutual exchange). Thus, *assimilation is human.*

Assimilation has been the nature of Bharat. There are many examples of assimilation of *people* in Bharat like Shaka, Hoona, Kushana etc.

Apart from this type of assimilation (of people), there have been other types of assimilation as well (of knowledge, instruments and systems, games, language etc.) in Bharat.

Knowledge—Astronomy (taken *Romak* from Rome, *Polish* from Alexandria in the name of a scientist Pole), Theatre (taken *Yavanika* from Yavanas), Medical Science (Allopathy, Homeopathy), Modern Technology etc.

Instruments and systems—Musical Instruments (Violin, Trumpet, Drum etc.), Systems (Rail, Auto Vehicles etc.).

Games—Hockey, Football, Cricket, Tennis etc.

Language—Various new words have been taken from other languages in all of the Bharatiya languages.

CONVERSION and HOME-COMING

Conversion has never been an issue in Bharat so long as it was amongst the religions originated in Bharat, such as Shaiva, Vaishnav, Jain, Bauddha, Sikh etc. (This can be referred to as 'conversion of first type'.) The reason is—such conversion does not change the mindset of the convert (*because of the similarities in the philosophy and world view of these religions*), it remains in the ambit of *Alsoism and Samaadara*. Therefore, the Sanskriti remains the same even after change in religion. However, it became a serious threat to our Sanskriti with the arrival of the Semitic religions like Islam and Christianity in Bharat and their efforts to convert the Hindus (belonging to all Hindu religions) by force or by hook and crook to their respective religion. (This can be referred to as 'conversion of second type'.) The reason is—such conversion changes the mindset of the convert from *Alsoism and Samaadara* to that of *Onlyism and Intolerance.* This amounts to change in Sanskriti as well, not confined just to change in religion. [*Precisely for this reason, Dr. Ambedkar, along with lakhs of his followers, embraced Bauddha religion (a religion originated in Bharat) instead of a Semitic religion (Christianity or Islam), when they resolved to convert. Also, it should be noted that the 'Niyogi*

Committee' constituted by the then Congress Govt in Madhya Pradesh, has recommended ban on religious conversions carried out by force, fraud or inducements in 1956 and the MP Govt has passed the 'Freedom of Religion Act 1968' (Dharma Swatantrya Adhiniyam 1968) based on the report of this Committee. Similar type of acts have been passed by Odisha and several other state Govts.] Therefore, it is said that this type of conversion amounts to change in nationality, because the nationality depends on Sanskriti.

Swami Vivekananda was very critical of this type of conversion. He used to say—"*Conversion of one Hindu is not just reducing the total number of Hindus by one, it also amounts to one more enemy.*" Mahatma Gandhi's opinion about this type of conversion is very clear from one of his statements—"*It is impossible for me to reconcile myself to the idea of conversion after the style that goes on in India*". Therefore, the Hindus try to bring back such converts into Hindu fold. This is *de-conversion*, popularly known as '*Home-Coming*' (Ghar Vaapasi).

Sometimes, the conversion of second type and home-coming both are equally criticised. This is not proper, because they are not similar. This type of conversion is iniquitous; because in a way, it is nothing but **Religious Imperialism** which is as bad as **Political Imperialism**. (*There is an opinion that Religious Imperialism is worse than Political Imperialism.*) On the other hand, home-coming is taking back a person who had been converted earlier, and hence, it is valid and right. (*Even if a person had been converted by conviction, the efforts for his/her home-coming are also valid; just as the conversion by conviction is considered as valid.*)

SANSKRITI and CULTURE

There is no appropriate word in English for the word 'Sanskriti' (just as there is no appropriate word in English for the word 'Dharma'). Usually, 'Culture' is taken as the English word for 'Sanskriti'. The word 'Culture' is derived from the word 'cult' which means a section of a religion. Therefore, the meaning of 'Culture' is 'behaviour of the people belonging to a particular cult'; which is not the meaning of 'Sanskriti'. Another meaning of culture is 'one that cultivates', but this as well does not represent the comprehensive meaning of 'Sanskriti'. Therefore, the word 'Sanskriti' should be used as it is in English, just as the word 'Dharma' is used as it is in it.

SANSKRITI and SABHYATA

Sometimes, the words 'Sanskriti' and 'Sabhyata'

(civilisation) are taken as *equivalent* and hence, they are considered as interchangeable. This is not proper, because their meanings are different.

Sabhyata gives an expression (*Abhivyakti*) to Sanskriti. Hence, Sabhyata may be different at different times because the expression depends on time, but Sanskriti remains same.

For example, cleanliness (inner and outward) is one of the values of Hindu Sanskriti. It has been brought in practice at different times by different means. (*The status of science and technology at different times has played a major role in having different means.*) For outward cleanliness, the means have been changing (*FROM* mop *TO* electric duster *TO* vacuum cleaner) and hence, they are referred to as *Mop civilisation, Electric Duster civilisation* and *Vacuum Cleaner civilisation*; but the Sanskriti is the same (Cleanliness) and hence, they are never referred to as *Mop culture* (the incorrect but frequently used word for *Sanskriti*), *Electric Duster culture* and *Vacuum Cleaner culture.*

[Same is true with the phrases 'Stone age civilisation', 'Bronze/Copper age civilisation' and 'Iron age civilisation'. They are never referred to as 'Stone age culture', 'Bronze/Copper age culture' and 'Iron age culture'.]

COMPOSITE SANSKRITI and SABHYATA

The phrases 'Composite Sanskriti' and 'Composite Sabhyata' are also taken as equivalent and hence, either of them is used assuming that they can be interchanged. However, this as well is not proper.

Let us take an example of a memorial constructed near the cremation place or burial of a well-known personality. The architecture of the memorial may be a mixture of the architectures of Bharat and Arab region. Therefore, it can be said that it is an example of *composite civilisation* of Bharat and Arab region. However, it is not an example of *composite Sanskriti*; because the dead body of that person was not half burned and half buried as a gesture to show belief in both Sanskritis (composite Sanskriti). It was either burned or buried. Thus, it can be seen that the Sabhyata can be—and usually is—composite, but the Sanskriti is not.

□

EPILOGUE

Dharma and Sanskriti are specific only to the human race, rest of the animate world follows its respective Prakriti.

Dharma is universal but every nation has its own Sanskriti to cater its needs and solve its problems. However, there is *humanity* in every human being and hence each Sanskriti ultimately strengthens humanity. This makes all of them integral (*Ekaatma*). It's a wonderful example of oneness in diversity and beauty can be and should be seen in it.

The end result of following Dharma (which is universal) and Sanskritis (which are diverse but integral) will be strengthening humanity and there will be *harmony without enmity* all over the world. However, the *condition precedent* is that Dharma and Sanskriti should be followed in *letter and spirit* everywhere. The persons who have realised this should not only pray for it, but also make sincere efforts to contribute their bit in this endeavour and make our wonderful mother earth a blissful place to live with happiness and peace.

~~

Every Hindu should not only understand the principles of Hindu Dharma and Sanskriti thoroughly, they should follow them in letter and spirit in their day-to-day personal, familial, professional and societal life. Then only one can be a *TRUE HINDU.*

Bharat has been a Vishwaguru not just because of the kings or monks or great personalities; in addition to them, it was a Vishwaguru because of the good character of common Hindus as well, who had gone to all parts of the world, which was reflected in everyone's conduct and behaviour. The people all over the world have learned several things from them, including an ideal way to lead life as a true human being, and hence, they could win their hearts and command their respect. For this reason, the world had given the status of a Vishwaguru to Bharat.

Presently, one can see all-round progress everywhere, but at the same time, the world is facing several grave problems (*ecological unbalance, lack of inner peace, growing intolerance and terrorism, finding a proper path of development which is eco-friendly and with human face, issue of globalisation with tremendous disparity, harmonising science and religion etc.*) and is looking for their solutions. The Hindu philosophy and world view (*and therefore, the Hindu Sanskriti*) are capable of providing solutions to all of such problems and could do so if the number of *TRUE HINDUS* is significantly large and then BHARAT could again acquire the status of a *VISHWAGURU* in the present-day context.

The compiler has made sincere efforts to explain Hindu Dharma and Sanskriti. Some of the readers may not agree with some of the points mentioned herein, but it should not be taken as a lacuna of Hindu Dharma and Sanskriti; it should be taken as a limitation of the compiler to adequately explain them. The compiler might have erred at a few places, for which he sincerely apologises.

This book doesn't encompass everything that falls within the ambit of Hindu Dharma and Sanskriti. It is too vast a subject to be covered within the size of this book. The purpose is to give the readers a glimpse of Hindu Dharma and Sanskriti and hopefully they would desire to know more about it.

The readers should not take the things given in this book as the ultimate words. Some high-level books may be referred to for that.

□□□